Penguin Crossword Puzzles
Series Editor: Alan Cash

The Seventh Penguin Book of *The Times* Crosswords

Also available:

The First Penguin Book of *The Times* Crosswords
The Second Penguin Book of *The Times* Crosswords
The Third Penguin Book of *The Times* Crosswords
The Fourth Penguin Book of *The Times* Crosswords
The Fifth Penguin Book of *The Times* Crosswords
The Sixth Penguin Book of *The Times* Crosswords
The Eighth Penguin Book of *The Times* Crosswords

The Seventh Penguin Book
of *The Times* Crosswords

Penguin Books

Penguin Books Ltd, Harmondsworth, Middlesex, England
Viking Penguin Inc., 40 West 23rd Street, New York, New York 10010, U.S.A.
Penguin Books Australia Ltd, Ringwood, Victoria, Australia
Penguin Books Canada Limited, 2801 John Street, Markham, Ontario, Canada L3R 1B4
Penguin Books (N.Z.) Ltd, 182–190 Wairau Road, Auckland 10, New Zealand

First published in book form by Penguin Books 1986
Reprinted 1986

Printed and bound in Great Britain by
Cox & Wyman Ltd, Reading
Filmset in Linotron Times by
Rowland Phototypesetting Ltd
Bury St Edmunds, Suffolk

Foreword

The sixty puzzles in this selection of *Times* crosswords appeared in the months from January to September 1983. They include the twenty-seven puzzles used in the annual *Times* Crossword Championship, which in 1983 was sponsored for the first time by Collins Dictionaries. The championship puzzles carry footnotes which, in the case of regional final and national final puzzles, indicate their relative difficulty by showing the proportion of competitors who solved the puzzles within the thirty minutes allowed for each (without the aid of reference books).

Those looking for a puzzle that is really testing should try Puzzle No. 60. This was the 1983 Eliminator Puzzle, designed to baffle most competitors so that the numbers of qualifiers could be reduced where these exceeded the accommodation available at the various regional finals. Only the least successful entries were eliminated. Reference books may be consulted. The solution given at the end of the book is followed by notes explaining all the clues.

> Edmund Akenhead
> Crossword Editor of *The Times* over the period
> of publication of these puzzles

The Puzzles

1

Across

1 First thing Abraham did to Isaac, for example, in a club (5)
4 The type of temptation London provides – drink (9)
9 Unlike Dogberry's comparisons, not to be sniffed at (9)
10 Paddy as the normal agriculture initially here (5)
11 Give loud cry of pain like a coward (6)
12 First seen round the border, African warrior bands (8)
14 Strength shown perhaps in one second bursts (10)
16 A boy's source of energy (4)
19 Support equal, we hear (4)
20 Astronomer incurs trouble after work in church (10)
22 Position of a striker (8)
23 Humperdinck in turn to some extent a singer (6)
26 Returning in the morning, has a mental derangement (5)
27 One might be the sum of two equal squares (9)
28 Saw this performed without screen adaptation (9)
29 An epic-making baseball feat (5)

Down

1 Bird-catcher's practical joke (5-4)
2 Greek bird makes a beastly noise (5)
3 Sailor loudly disapproves hard type of headgear (8)
4 Blessed if Macbeth could say it! (4)
5 Expert needed to get us beyond the turbulent stream (4, 6)
6 Like the city of New York's dress style? (6)
7 Fall, so we hear, to Athenian weapon? (9)
8 The poet Shelley's Adonais (5)
13 Champion golfer's casual request to caddie? (3, 3, 4)
15 The sort of milk Pooh, after honey, hoped to avoid (9)
17 Warrior Sam Small (ex-Holloway) (9)
18 Eating corn perhaps, each appears to transgress (8)
21 Ship's planking supplied by canonised libertine (6)
22 Many in a revolutionary situation ready to fight (5)
24 Muslim lady looks to be a sticker (5)
25 But can these cakes sell like hot ones? (4)

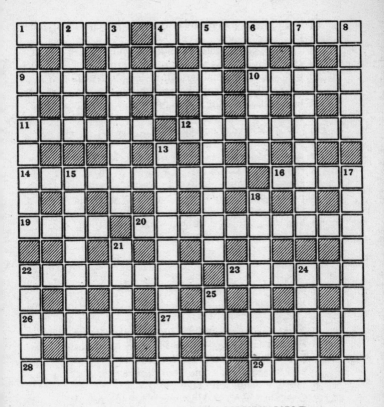

This was the qualifying puzzle for the 1983 *COLLINS DICTIONARIES Times Crossword Championship.*

2

Across

1 Take Bill to church parking by the square (6)
4 How crocodiles travel? (3, 2, 3)
10 On promotion sailor has given up former vice (7)
11 City-dwellers often bold in speech? (7)
12 Right to a cavern perhaps in an old Indian state (10)
13 German boy bearing coin from Cyprus (4)
15 Like Juvenal's work – or old Greek drama, say? (7)
17 Actually it may not be legal (2, 5)
19 Spray a damaged rose and see a return (7)
21 Fence in French playing-field (7)
23 In Scotland go for the workers' group (4)
24 Composer gives the old king a drink (4, 6)
27 Millet production once meant a bit of money to us (7)
28 Player giving a sound but mechanical performance (7)
29 Producers of graceful children (8)
30 Stout or wine left to head of Y M C A (6)

Down

1 A saint as a false model for a Grand Duchess (9)
2 Military leader and politician come to measure of agreement (7)
3 It's always so icy-cold in the Underground! (10)
5 Checkpoint for vehicles say at Surrey river-crossing? (9)
6 In Italy singer lacks tone (4)
7 This lance figures in another Michelangelo work (7)
8 The bird on the left's no use! (5)
9 Combined parties taking care of pound's rise (4)
14 With aid of a coin perhaps we get a fan (10)
16 A summons – sort of lousy unfeeling way to treat us (9)
18 Dressed to go in for dinner? (4-5)
20 Break promise to M. Clair and guest? No way! (7)
22 The detachment's not in position (7)
23 General assignment (5)
25 See opening for estate agent (4)
26 Smelly old one perhaps (4)

4

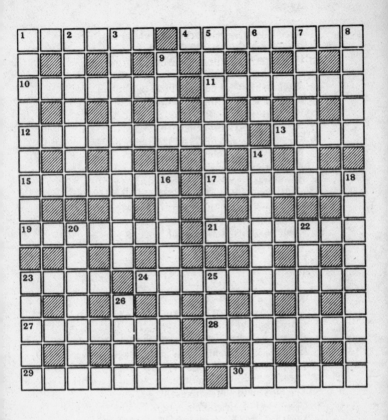

3

Across

1 Offers more doubt, is uncertain (7)
5 Violent sounding Scotsman, a bully (7)
9 Bond seen in the distance (5)
10 No vitamin A about? A number lost energy (9)
11 Claim a lock back, one in progress (9)
12 Asserted loudly 'It could be worse!' (5)
13 Crowd took to the road (5)
15 Close a road in pernickety environs (9)
18 Stayed in bed – 'older of gun (9)
19 Old London river boats (5)
21 Schismatic Adriatic town (5)
23 Club about to provide support (9)
25 Fetch coal in the new-fangled way, it's cleaner (4-5)
26 Writer George returned to French island (5)
27 Fish beat its victim (7)
28 Repartee of the ropiest sort (7)

Down

1 Monster difficult to see for the trees (7)
2 Fungus resembling frog-spawn, say? (9)
3 Victor loses his head in the ring (5)
4 Victoria perhaps, with 'er paper supplier (9)
5 Water is said to be king (5)
6 Where the standard is high (9)
7 Jones the building (5)
8 Conventionally but half defines it (7)
14 Vehicle enters say in climbing event (6, 3)
16 Airmen follow up to take in the sponsor (9)
17 The regimen is, I detect, unusual (9)
18 Dwarf liable to hit out? (7)
20 Start and finish of act seen in there (7)
22 Half in love with a substitute (5)
23 Spoil by holding up excessively (5)
24 John Hornblower's raised us from this (5)

4

Across

1 Cheeky sort of complaint? (4-4)
5 Main type of fastener (6)
10 Confound with a heavy blow (5)
11 Honest supporter in the field (6, 3)
12 Change is kept to middle of traffic, that's plain (9)
13 Control of sale, say, of this paper (5)
14 Soldier suffered pain when extended (7)
16 I R A formation was first to be reviled (6)
19 So recompense retired draughtsman? (6)
21 Excuse being quiet about the preacher's theme (7)
23 Stupid Roman triumvir dismissed us (5)
25 Sea fever – remedy includes a fast (9)
27 Avoid committing oneself to accelerando (9)
28 Retired doctor holds up about one drug (5)
29 One betting cautiously to include the field? (6)
30 Allotted as subscribed (8)

Down

1 Young girls once in a panic? (8)
2 Eccentric patient in car (9)
3 Mount named by Dumas (5)
4 One in the family appears to be conservative (7)
6 Revolver left behind by soccer fan (9)
7 Beat the seeds? (5)
8 Figures in rows (6)
9 This old boy's at the end of the line (6)
15 Our mutual friend's character shown here in the churchyard? (9)
17 Topping performance (9)
18 Flowed right into the new Tees dam (8)
20 Eastern robber gives party – it includes airman (6)
21 Pilgrims cheating at cards? (7)
22 People absorbed in local activities? (6)
24 Equipped to shoot with members (5)
26 Ruthless? Never this Biblical character (5)

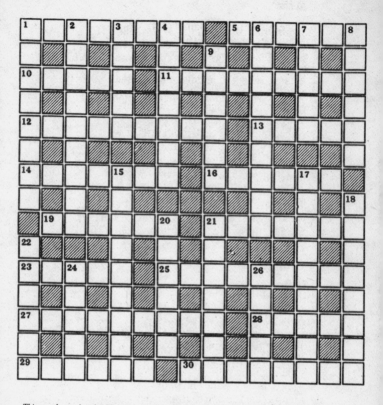

This puzzle, used at the Glasgow regional final of the COLLINS DICTIONARIES Times Crossword Championship, was solved within 30 minutes by 45 per cent of the finalists.

5

Across

1 Sailor's receiving a primate – pert fellow (10)
6 An artist leaves Miss Allen a horse (4)
9 Witness this at a Soho club and dine out for a change (10)
10 Former ruler – some pasha, he? (4)
12 Within easy reach, like Cratchit's employer at first (4)
13 Make Con run the club (9)
15 Thus descended, due perhaps to loneliness (8)
16 How to overcome the fires of thirst (6)
18 Become less stern, having repeated the advance (6)
20 Unsophisticated institution's play on words (8)
23 Party workers? (9)
24 Choice of keys for central part (4)
26 Smack back of this little pest (4)
27 Durability of certain waves, it's suggested (10)
28 Increase the height, say, of these beams (4)
29 Many have no alternative – ring the porter (4-6)

Down

1 Green horse? (4)
2 To keep secret, formerly, in California (7)
3 Language of arithmetician among the ferns (6, 6)
4 'O Attic shape! Fair ____!' (Keats) (8)
5 A departure from the book (6)
7 Each modification in articles belonging to ancient Greece (7)
8 Live with a couple of workers in arrears (10)
11 Tacit agreement to make aircraftman rest (12)
14 Old Moore a good man – jolly lad? Look into that (10)
17 One who goes about returning service – flimsy stuff! (8)
19 Sufficient room for Prospero's dukedom (7)
21 Food item father's pin-up found about right (7)
22 To this the outcome could be three-love (6)
25 Dam is almost like Macbeth's sisters (4)

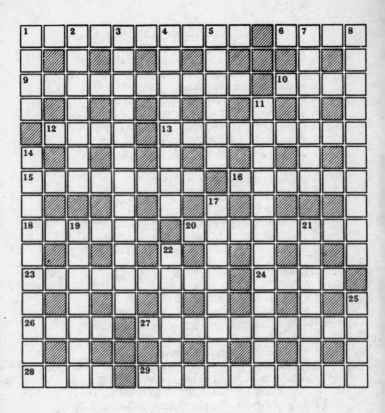

6

Across

1 Perhaps, sir, it could be cure (with 24) (6, 6)
9 Support large numbers of sappers (9)
10 Cold house brings one endless melancholy (5)
11 Exam for Alexander and Alfred? (6)
12 Nothing in extra enclosure is exposed (4, 4)
13 Princess who fell for neat trick, by Zeus! (6)
15 Scottish speciality contains meat for alfresco meal (8)
18 Powerful feller observed on the links (5-3)
19 Plant growing wild in porch, I see (6)
21 Too particular, finding nothing right in merchant's city (8)
23 Insect about to secrete sort of acid (6)
26 Skin is damaged by knife first (5)
27 Supreme horse from Brazilian state (9)
28 Novel student achieved quick result from his experiment (12)

Down

1 Craft of religious scoundrel (7)
2 Lift to take to ground level with one in (5)
3 The point of this device may not be apparent (6-3)
4 Not all the player has to learn? (4)
5 Puck seen flying over this polar area? (3-5)
6 Rotter and I going in opposite directions (5)
7 A Liberal leader S D P has troubled recklessly (8)
8 Born overweight baby may show resilience (6)
14 Sergeant ordered to give detective chemicals (8)
16 Day commemorating saint's ending of war (9)
17 Thrown by the Duchess's cook (as cheeky Tinker Bell might do) (8)
18 Best denied to beggars, they say (6)
20 Laconic skill shown in bridge (7)
22 Upset about child – it's a big blow (5)
24 A refusal to recognise English accent (5)
25 Berliner's odd bits of cheese (4)

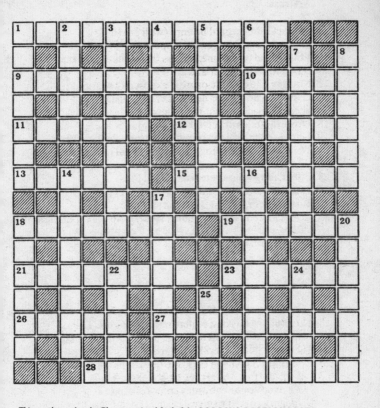

This puzzle, used at the Glasgow regional final of the COLLINS DICTIONARIES Times Crossword Championship, was solved within 30 minutes by 35 per cent of the finalists.

7

Across

1 Insect knowing about one little 2 (7)
5 False claim about American show (7)
9 Small and mischievous? For Spaniards it's the end! (5)
10 Sweet drink with coolant (9)
11 Stephen the first to give spoil to Norse war-god (6)
12 Outside study, schoolgirl gets the wrong end of the stick (8)
14 Guide is a good person always (5)
15 Reptile with an attachment occasionally to pears (9)
18 Grannie's letters are rambling and full of dry gossip (9)
20 Provided by 1 across not weighing much (5)
22 Straddle most superior horse (8)
24 Celebrity goes round, say, a lot of soldiers (6)
26 Nice flag (9)
27 Bones of a king 1972 years ago (5)*
28 Long-lasting love leaves laboured involvement (7)
29 Getting on like a 25? (7)

Down

1 Forenames unusual in a lodger? (9)
2 He can award penalty point twice after a 13 (7)
3 Like Miss Day before her engagement to Dick Dewy (5-4)
4 The old record 'Cry' (4)
5 Many a writer takes time with make-up (10)
6 One who should be prepared for scorn (5)
7 Dickens's fireside game? (7)
8 A town's vegetables (5)
13 Implore and maybe get deified, for instance (10)
16 Plant's stake touched by Midas? (9)
17 Composed, so they say, a French song lacking heart and all-round quality (9)
19 Artiste could be more attractive (7)
21 Youth leader accepts a pound in foreign currency (7)
22 As a cricketer, Edward is restrained (5)

*This puzzle was published in 1983.

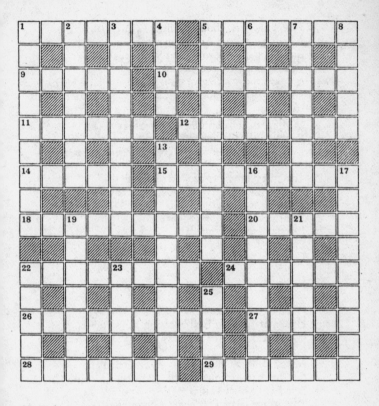

23 To get a lozenge, take letter to a Greek doctor (5)
25 A bit of wood put in the boot (4)

8

Across

1 College boat, but not for bumping races (5)
4 Led by Mrs Mopp, the French beat this fraud (9)
9 Bulldog-like action – sue for damages (9)
10 Mark was almost canned (5)
11 Noddy as alias for this dwarf? (6)
12 Lady is twice involved in blood purification (8)
14 'He who . . . leaped fondly into Etna flames' (10)
16 Writings include nothing for 'cryptogam' (4)
19 Poet telling of 14 lost £500 in the river (4)
20 I silently consent to accept copper recently immunised (10)
22 Trinity's symbol not really a diamond (8)
23 Press, within limits of 1 across, for a flag (6)
26 Loves to devour a book, Architectural Moulding (5)
27 A tortoise-hedgehog combine? Just so (9)
28 Busman marking time? (9)
29 Problem for a jockey (5)

Down

1 Female city graduate gave birth to a king (9)
2 Queen of the Near East? Possibly not so near (5)
3 Gaol-break receives publicity as frolicsome adventure (8)
4 Nancy Bell's penultimate survivor died in Hawaii (4)
5 Not being there holding money implies no drinks (10)
6 A trifle like Miss Muffet (6)
7 That which conveys vehement emotion (9)
8 Bridge partners take in one date in Rome (5)
13 Break-down of the figures expected from him? (10)
15 Singular nether-wear on the world stage (9)
17 Digs up round the border of the battlefield (9)
18 Swimmer appears to be thrashing about (8)
21 Ordinary moderate luxuries, H Q supplying decoration (6)
22 He thus holds to austerity (5)
24 As cold as eels, say? (5)
25 Astronomer, poet, tent-maker (4)

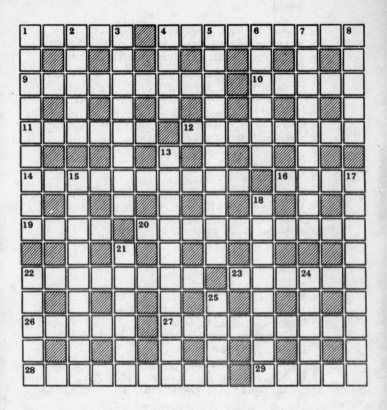

This puzzle, used at the Glasgow regional final of the COLLINS DICTIONARIES
Times Crossword Championship, was solved within 30 minutes by 26 per cent of the finalists.

9

Across

1 Model beginning to pose has very poor clothing (7)
5 Sort of turn in East London which is widely admired (7)
9 Saint takes first-class return from Balkan country (5)
10 Wait outside Ascot for a change of clothing (9)
11 Overflowing with joy at new UN beer-tax (9)
12 Wager gold when backing, like a sovereign (5)
13 I don't get mixed up with gossip (2, 3)
15 Charming utterance but inflammable (9)
18 Plot extended to cover a bunk? (9)
19 Virile Scot helped leader, nothing more (5)
21 Stop or pass on (5)
23 Not even a soldier (9)
25 Usually mother is a supporter of independence (4-5)
26 What wakes us up in jolly style (5)
27 Work for Labour, for example (7)
28 Make out record given with key to Navy (7)

Down

1 Harmless pill, gratifyingly effective? (7)
2 About to spring on journalist, but recoiled (9)
3 Information about art-form (5)
4 Modern house for an Englishman in the North-East (9)
5 Purpose of police duty (5)
6 Simon pretended to get ribbon (9)
7 Before end of day diver becomes crazy (5)
8 Chatterbox a sort of government notice made nervous (7)
14 The game is to upset mine with union backing (3, 3, 3)
16 Badly behaved mongrel (9)
17 It's a 'cello arrangement for swing (9)
18 A god is said to be our supporter (7)
20 As bowman he'd be in the forefront of a row (7)
22 A refreshing if unsatisfactory type of answer (5)
23 Singular bridge achievement in the Muslim world (5)
24 Type of snake in a stage menagerie? (5)

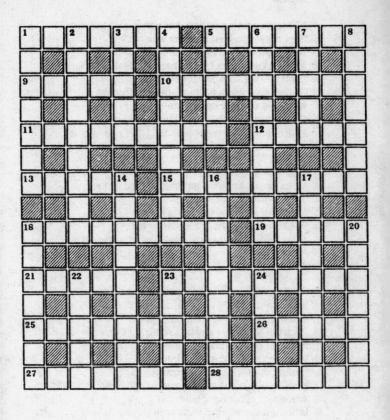

10

Across

1 Is distressed, internally affected by sea-food (6)
4 He does regular training (8)
10 Seconds are tense (9)
11 A girl could be made the object of chivalrous attention (5)
12 One more empty pollen-container (7)
13 Weary of military duty (7)
14 Left, in other words, at home to oversleep (3, 2)
15 In this, somehow, confining the Italian revolutionary (8)
18 Regressive church admits it's become stuck with dignity (8)
20 Trains one or two (5)
23 Make music with one instrument, not 5 (7)
25 Sort of swallow one drink (7)
26 Colour of fruit doesn't begin to vary (5)
27 Behave amorously and caress a bird (9)
28 Something to sit on to support the players (8)
29 A horse, in short, with an unkempt mane? (6)

Down

1 Becoming a blue, it's different (8)
2 With happy heart ramble, O K? (7)
3 Rod and cane broken accidentally (9)
5 Whence came Wombles, in the singular (3, 2, 3, 6)
6 Could possibly appear in strength (5)
7 It could be great as a means of riot control (4-3)
8 Wave that produces a wave (6)
9 18 indication of disapproval (2, 3, 3, 6)
16 Clue needed here for 'Way out' (9)
17 People I join with servility (8)
19 Girl can put up a calendar (7)
21 A big noise in concealment that's permanent (7)
22 Brash lad embraces female spirit (6)
24 Dangerous rocks? Shortens sail (5)

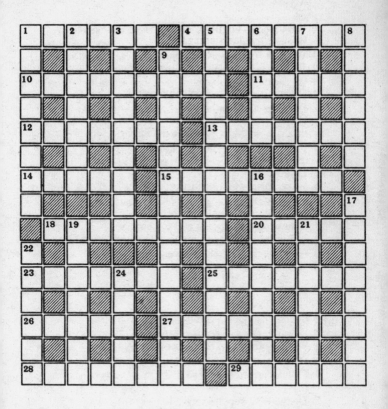

This puzzle, used at the Glasgow regional final of the COLLINS DICTIONARIES
Times Crossword Championship, was solved within 30 minutes by 60 per cent of the finalists.

11

Across

1 'White Girl' Verdi composed – seeker for sunken treasure (5-5)
9 Where to pick up some tropical bug, and antidote (6)
10 Butch type seen round the roads, driving cattle (8)
11 Be careful to receive Governor Edward (4, 4)
12 Man in church, say? (4)
13 Made fresh alteration to instrument without notice, right? (10)
15 How office bosses lay down the law (7)
17 No end of a baby, this balladmonger (7)
20 Various clients accept that French is in the melting-pot (10)
21 Artist owns about fifty (4)
23 Water plant by the mountain loved by a Trojan prince (8)
25 It may lead to marriage for a river girl (8)
26 Story about the race is just gossip (6)
27 Disconcerting if he's taken your watch, for instance (5-5)

Down

2 Key to picture-puzzle – a volcano (6)
3 Fragrant hand-out landlord's due to receive (8)
4 Philosopher destroyed its decorum (10)
5 Helping a fish to sort of travel, name this fin (7)
6 Goods carrier loses head in the main body of also-rans (4)
7 Disturb – by repatriating colonists? (8)
8 Shaw's heroine upset by applicants (10)
12 Without the Spanish entry, show is lacking refinement (10)
14 Has this company some connection with cattle? (5-5)
16 Flirtatious type of bird took food, some say (8)
18 Rustic asks if this monster is one of Titania's attendants (8)
19 It's right to pass and fall back (7)
22 Pope's man, say, comes in after time (6)
24 'Then fall, Caesar!' (4)

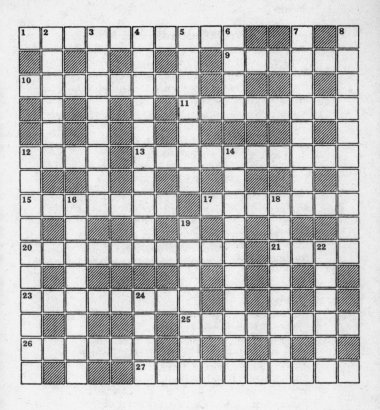

12

Across

1 Carpeting, a top covering on the floor (8, 4)
9 Water carrier used to be very good in Indian tent, mostly (5-4)
10 Bowler out for a duck? (5)
11 Plenty for Pussy (6)
12 Allowing Drummond to hold nothing after the high note (8)
13 More offensive in private (6)
15 Boss of a colliery in Somerset (8)
18 Belts you violently and insensitively (8)
19 Container ship (6)
21 One of two passed in common entrance (8)
23 Horrified Turkish commander, a good man (6)
26 It's futile to write back in Italian (5)
27 Leader of German army left general resembling Caesar at Philippi (5-4)
28 Putting to sleep thus in hospital; typical only after treatment (12)

Down

1 Faites vos jeux, old lady (7)
2 Break lease and make a stand (5)
3 Mere members used to lift heavy weights (5-4)
4 There's nothing about a fix (4)
5 Scottish river tartan is cunningly contrived (4-4)
6 Withholding literally the fourth dimension? (5)
7 Falsely they say you accused Hermes the carrier of it (8)
8 Means the Ministry of Defence is wrong (6)
14 Gas or metal turning up low-down (8)
16 Vigorous men don't start to work before call-up (9)
17 Is one blinded by this weapon? (5-3)
18 Appoint a hearing for a yellow foreigner (6)
20 Draw only half an animal inside (7)
22 Receptacle that's cracked (5)
24 The spirit of a sailor described by Browning (5)
25 Make tracks and fast (4)

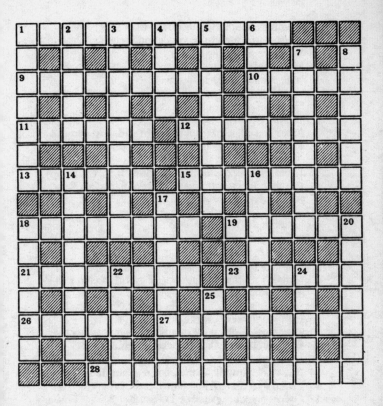

This puzzle, used at the Leeds regional final of the COLLINS DICTIONARIES Times Crossword Championship, was solved within 30 minutes by 15 per cent of the finalists.

13

Across

1 Records a score, from Bayeux? (8)
5 Nurse performing as a muscle-binder (6)
10 What are you doing here? (9, 6)
11 Money advanced by one member to all the others (7)
12 X as put in Greece against wine (7)
13 Incline to wither, in general (8)
15 'auls a bit of the roof (5)
18 Bound to be shifty (5)
20 Mock some backward, but quite lucid, Irishmen (8)
23 Heard you leaving funny peculiar copy (7)
25 Sink the man who started it (7)
26 Ultima Thule, for instance, as clue for D? (3, 4, 2, 6)
27 Cut, in other words, the start of your article (6)
28 Adapted the story of Anne's home (8)

Down

1 Alarm at hearing of poison (6)
2 Miranda's father lost nothing; Edward too did well (9)
3 Temporarily stop us turning up to pay out (7)
4 Equation's solution includes pole or perch (5)
6 Learned to make crooked die true (7)
7 Take forty winks, then finally a smaller number (5)
8 Most resembling Canning's knife-grinder (8)
9 Money indeed, not starting 6 (8)
14 Puts aside Antony, in the loan he requested (8)
16 Loved to redesign capital race-track (9)
17 Graces one out of many good causes (8)
19 Inscription – record it over Herbert (7)
21 Most unrefined of French bread around (7)
22 Man of the week? (6)
24 Edgar Allan's the last to decry verse (5)
25 Firework symphony? (5)

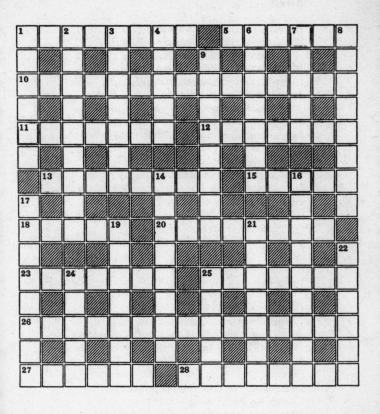

14

1 But poor Rasputin was not of their persuasion (8)
5 Webster once taught Robert a lesson (6)
10 A lot of paper money in this province (5)
11 Historian wanders into Ely tavern (9)
12 Hybrid of second class buried outside (9)
13 Is unable to love some poetry (5)
14 Trouble about letters in a marginal note (7)
16 Delightful as Tennyson's fair women (6)
19 Like a bird following a ship? (6)
21 Solvent colonist? (7)
23 Baptist joined with a rich gentleman of this city (5)
25 Religious type – one of Indo-European origin, say (9)
27 No complicated fee for this, the tenth legal point? (9)
28 His music halls were marble (5)
29 'He bravely broach'd his boiling bloody——'
   (*A Midsummer Night's Dream*) (6)
30 Excuses for holy man's return after worrying expert (8)

Down

1 Guerrilla weapon (8)
2 Chemical processes making coarse tin (9)
3 West Country flower for the army to spoil (5)
4 Old city in part of South Africa unspoiled by man (7)
6 Forewarned of being confined, inwardly cries unhappily
   (9)
7 Same money for the senior member (5)
8 Chance for Roderick (6)
9 Submission on such low joints, perhaps (6)
15 Is Isaacson right to be in so informative a book? (9)
17 Not a prime number – a number of many parts (9)
18 Royalty in tax after polling system (8)
20 Not without an expression of disgust for a poor score (6)
21 Rough ripples cause drag (7)
22 Coolness of a doctor for some Palestinians? (6)
24 No, nothing missing in fish ball (5)
26 Part of the morning circuit? (5)

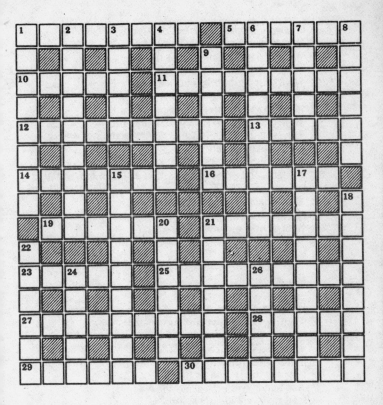

This puzzle, used at the Leeds regional final of the COLLINS DICTIONARIES Times Crossword Championship, was solved within 30 minutes by 18 per cent of the finalists.

15

Across

1 Dogmatic French governor, legislator and 20 (10)
6 Doctor leaves capital by boat (4)
9 Warmer, in the main (4, 6)
10 Sign of batting failures? (4)
12 What we no longer have to eat (4)
13 Like a measure in a volume for star-gazers (9)
15 Hated cricket indeed! (8)
16 Place to stay about south of this one (6)
18 Proverbially tearful, Misses Bo-Peep and Locket? (6)
20 Convivial politician? (5-3)
23 Sort of plug about pupil that's very bright (9)
24 'Sweet _____ sweetest nymph that liv'st unseen' (Milton) (4)
26 The bisexual Spanish girl? (4)
27 He would stick up for his employer (10)
28 Kind of help in office (4)
29 Some bounder going to seed? (6-4)

Down

1 Quiet time for bookmaker (4)
2 Trusting in wild talk about priest (7)
3 Outstanding performance one of six of the best at school? (12)
4 Sailor gets his support from old medicine (3-5)
5 News centre in Venice (6)
7 A rotten lot going over the border? (7)
8 Country one Liddell explored (10)
11 Best soft drink featured on TV? (3, 2, 3, 4)
14 Young fellow's climb to receive hand-out (10)
17 Ant-eater long troubled in physical distress (8)
19 A boat for every customer present (7)
21 Holy leader takes cover between scholars (7)
22 Limited penalty includes it (6)
25 Said to be partly demoralised (4)

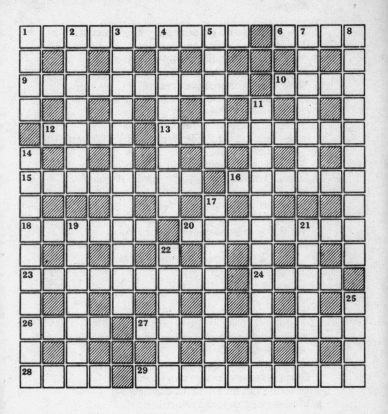

Across

1 Rule from South-East wanted by its nationalists? Just the reverse (5)
4 Deep depression – full of drink, perhaps (5-4)
9 Unassailable counterpart of Papal bull? (6, 3)
10 More than one enthusiast shines (5)
11 What highwaymen do is, with respect, unprofessional (6)
12 No time to start an operation? (4, 4)
14 Like deeds of a traitor beheaded – that's fair (10)
16 Chancy way to raise a little money (4)
19 Wise old Greek doesn't reach conclusion on his own (4)
20 Opera, if not funny, might be grand (10)
22 Into which Lord Lundy was shoved 'towards the age of twenty-six' (Belloc) (8)
23 Sort of chaser that will do for hunt (6)
26 Not abridged like some new books (5)
27 Nine so-called Popes, including the English one (9)
28 Get to the pass somehow with expedition (4-5)
29 Ground swells? (5)

Down

1 Young man advised to go thus from Harrow to Oxford? (9)
2 Happy old Scotswoman (5)
3 Changes to another's style of furniture (8)
4 Prepare cases for a collection of suits (4)
5 Fresh enthusiasm, and source of 15 (3, 7)
6 Wealthy man supports bit of fireside chat (3-3)
7 Not on green, perhaps, yet below par (3, 6)
8 Install a serious piece of scientific equipment (5)
13 Vehicle at school? That's one way to travel (5, 5)
15 Fifteen involved in perfect display of potter's skill (3, 6)
17 Marshals? They have a job handling crooks (9)
18 Pursuing first part of 15, despite everything (5, 3)
21 Running problem a streaker doesn't have (6)
22 Just like Bunter to take fruit pie that's missing (5)
24 It detects a bandit coming up or going down (5)
25 This dog's a point above the rest, we hear (4)

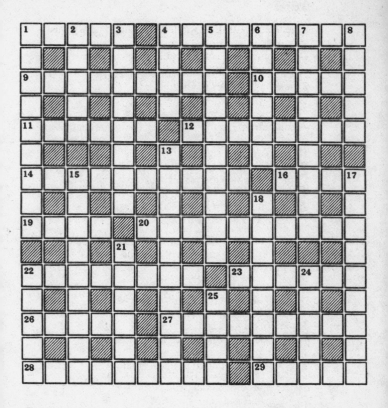

This puzzle, used at the Leeds regional final of the *COLLINS DICTIONARIES Times Crossword Championship*, was solved within 30 minutes by 47 per cent of the finalists.

17

Across

1 Monster giving a headsman little satisfaction (5)
4 String mislaid by Sir Arthur (4, 5)
9 Perfume distilled to touch a lip (9)
10 Not like sound from synod altercation (5)
11 Banned union does not need this (8-7)
12 Delicacy one caught in Tyne, perhaps (6)
14 Girl in this Latin embrace is all Greek (8)
17 A conundrum, result of selecting the initial characters (8)
19 Has a steep exchange rate (6)
22 Wordy diet for one hoping to go to law (6, 4, 5)
24 Capital for which toy-maker receives approval (5)
25 These towns were in league with the Germans (9)
26 Almost the wind of Hamlet's madness (3-6)
27 Loner forced to become member (5)

Down

1 Its victim may hop in a frenzy (9)
2 Some cleaners are so off-putting to chaps (5)
3 In a race he is an ungodly type (7)
4 Room for a thrust? Nothing in it (6)
5 About 100 foolish fellows in the British Isles (8)
6 Laconic form of weather signals (7)
7 Might be fired if I ignored this regulation (9)
8 Make deep research as Adam was wont to do (5)
13 One cautious in play? (9)
15 First-class state (9)
16 Rebound, from a glance? (8)
18 How would Thorndike's doctor deal with a fainting fit? (7)
20 Get utmost out of broken meter (7)
21 This cash return would do for a junket (6)
22 Emma's suitor gave change for a pound note (5)
23 It spins and lifts both ways (5)

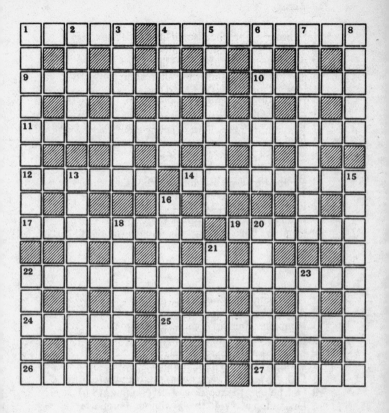

18

Across

1 Caught a bird that's black or yellow (6)
4 Some amphibians captured shortly without delay (8)
10 This honest fellow will never ring false (9)
11 Student pursuing exotic beast is a kind of nut (5)
12 Old soldier raced to ruin (7)
13 Hence turkeys and not people (7)
14 Band of citizens drinking beer supplied by him (5)
15 Points scored by Pakistani runner showing diligence (8)
18 Honest art is rejected in a sense (8)
20 On which pirates aim to rule the waves . . . (5)
23 . . . but never thus to master us (7)
25 Bender that goes to a lady's head (7)
26 This goose found in London (5)
27 Form of speech heard, I see, in logical debate (9)
28 Leather has changed colour (8)
29 Bumble's bugle perhaps, the French variety (6)

Down

1 A blinding fall of water? (8)
2 A sequence was first put up in Sussex (7)
3 Plant hire a pub arranged – nothing in it (9)
5 Fugitive captain one of spirited courage? (6, 8)
6 Like Philip as an appeal judge (5)
7 Surpass with gold in such sports (7)
8 Dog ails terribly when out of this country (6)
9 One helping to provide cast-off clothing? (8-6)
16 Divination of a kind that is without a supporter (9)
17 Rich once, constructing this coast road (8)
19 Metric measures set up for a bit of mosaic (7)
21 Like an agent with authority placed in a document (7)
22 Island Byron's singer burned to leave? (6)
24 Moving a prison (5)

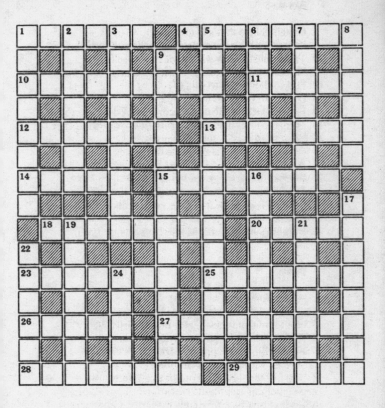

This puzzle, used at the Leeds regional final of the COLLINS DICTIONARIES Times Crossword Championship, was solved within 30 minutes by 37 per cent of the finalists.

19

Across

1 Remained restrained (7)
5 Bravo, perhaps, gets one bill after another (7)
9 Dead right? Not now (5)
10 Innocent allurement of small fry (9)
11 Was in time for about anything (6)
12 Act to cover the renegade (8)
14 To be seen in some part like Falstaff (5)
15 Passing, sees Ian's in trouble in the river (9)
18 Real meaning of wealth (9)
20 At full speed in a German river (5)
22 Words of reproof about poor Rose from teacher (8)
24 Brown's back in time to become a family man (6)
26 About to enter seaside sport, taking the air (9)
27 Honey-badger can be 9 (5)
28 Gun in a mess – work round with Chinese varnish (4, 3)
29 Bore, in conclusion, was uncommonly rude (7)

Down

1 Love is casual, loose, and lustful (9)
2 Thrust forward, and died loyal, capturing 500 (7)
3 Churchmen in divorce? You could write on it! (9)
4 In adversity, drink (4)
5 Soured about one getting flattered all round (10)
6 Completely cold and unproductive (5)
7 Eager to appear in one Scottish mystical interpretation (7)
8 Paid – about to put up a musical work (5)
13 One way and another, bad. Stop! (10)
16 Astounded – not all at the same time (9)
17 Sweet girl, well-adjusted all round, went underground (9)
19 Part one bird from another (7)
21 Nemesis, unfortunately, takes a high place (7)
22 Apocryphal Jew gets 12½ cents to start with (5)
23 Proportion not all share (5)
25 S-bend? What the Yank might say (4)

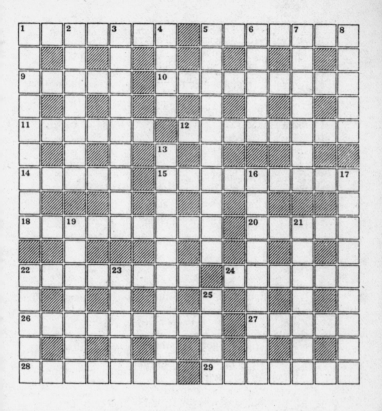

20

Across

1 Argentine taking cover where stars are shining (6, 6)
9 Hunter's slogan? (9)
10 What some players read others hope to make (5)
11 So this result means no cold consommé (6)
12 In a small volume aimed for revision – merely theoretical (8)
13 Another 9 in the kitchen garden (6)
15 Main prospect here having left awkward situation (8)
18 What a divine compact! (8)
19 Johnson the lexicographer, a harmless one (6)
21 He suffered in Hades where spirits are imprisoned (8)
23 Tom and East meet Superwitch! (6)
26 Petrarch's inspiration in monastic cells (5)
27 Discount included for a bad hat (9)
28 Medical applications aren't commonly made by one so virtuous (7, 5)

Down

1 Noticed deposit left on furniture made by carpenters (7)
2 Food for the idle unruly louts (5)
3 Kipling character gave the leopard 4s. (9)
4 See 3 (4)
5 Editor one with a part to play behind the iron curtain (8)
6 Relaxed while the river rose outside (5)
7 Absinth for Screwtape's nephew (8)
8 Secure, otherwise set free (6)
14 Elijah's food suppliers hold nothing high class for the very hungry (8)
16 Electric rays discharged from tubes (9)
17 Asks if three quarters include a number of sheets (8)
18 Stock of blue ribbon with sort of lace trimming (6)
20 Earth's essential part (7)
22 Benefit of a tip once (5)
24 Mites seen about in the swirling air (5)
25 Fellow apparently receives weapon seconds offered (4)

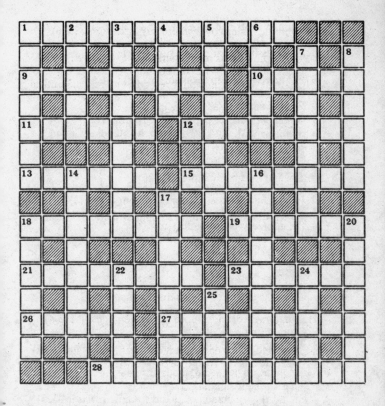

This puzzle, used at the Bristol regional final of the COLLINS DICTIONARIES Times Crossword Championship, was solved within 30 minutes by 26 per cent of the finalists.

21

Across

1 Emma's contrived to get husband, I note – foreign title for her? (8)
5 Like Cassius apparently getting article out of Communist country (6)
8 Achieve security in the main by a fluke (4, 6)
9 Change 22 up to and including U S version (4)
10 E.g. Tower of Pisa? (6, 8)
11 Quality of doubles pair won sets, perhaps (7)
13 Being printed, unlike 'Far from the Madding Crowd' (2, 5)
15 Peculiar sort of case for a policeman (7)
18 Makes, for instance, a fuss (7)
21 County bigwig found on board (8, 6)
22 Judges' final sentence – then this compassion (4)
23 Making impact, I am, with papers I have shown (10)
24 His master wrote so badly (6)
25 Attempt to return service with hesitation, being very light (8)

Down

1 Something worthless, note, seen when tide ebbs (3-4)
2 Cynthia's mood is novel (9)
3 A revolting type, Jack, joins me in college (7)
4 Nightmare in Cantabrigian transport (7)
5 Alcoholic on boat – he stands firm (4-5)
6 Smarter shade of blue (7)
7 Extraordinary humbug unlikely to cause reaction (4, 3)
12 Striking successes – one way to get this? (5, 4)
14 Policy concerned with ends, not means? (9)
16 Constable, perhaps, put in this by informer (7)
17 He had an uncle and sisters on the stage (7)
18 Parting word to comfort a legendary cow-girl (7)
19 Paul was here – epistle he's written to us (7)
20 Female speculator more deadly than male (3-4)

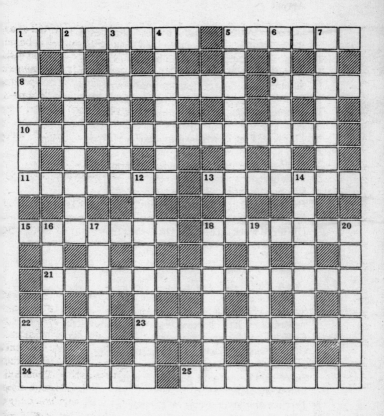

22

Across

1 Stable conditions required by his consul designate? (8)
5 See me backing horse entered in Derby, for example (6)
10 National leader once hidden by flags (5)
11 Occasional butt from goat following girl (5, 4)
12 Scoundrel leading current stoppage in port (9)
13 Poplar's Liberal entering a working alliance (5)
14 Source of appeal that isn't answered? (7)
16 A sort of din, in short (6)
19 17, divided into parts by grammarians (6)
21 Girl as model, or some lad perhaps (7)
23 Have these bones one point in common? (5)
25 Firm decisions made here to embark into space (9)
27 Writer – or forger (9)
28 Oh! I see you are pronounced out of order – that's rare (5)
29 Desire to work second shift in T-shirt (6)
30 Potboy who succeeded girl in shebeen (8)

Down

1 Squeeze applied in Health Service (8)
2 A certain trick to produce a rise for everybody (4, 5)
3 Beau getting magnanimous sign from French (5)
4 Club for boatmen with one in front holding pole (7)
6 Safeguard rare metal (9)
7 Stone dam perpetually producing water (5)
8 Funny chap, old Joe (6)
9 Terrible employer, Peter or Thomas (6)
15 Jams round motorway may lead to certain arguments (9)
17 Devils-on-horseback found here, so to speak? (9)
18 Ancient philosopher making annual appearance (3, 5)
20 Small fellow booked, somehow not like his creator (6)
21 Eccentric, turning up Her Majesty on a foreign coin (7)
22 John was such a clever statesman (6)
24 Capital invested in 1857 (5)
26 Why, we hear, supporting bones may appear dangerous (5)

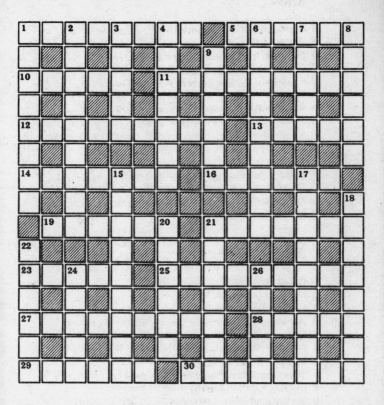

This puzzle, used at the Bristol regional final of the COLLINS DICTIONARIES Times Crossword Championship, was solved within 30 minutes by 8 per cent of the finalists.

23

Across

1 Footballer gets the bird for cheeky repartee (8)
5 A spring appears to be plentiful (6)
9 Manage to redesign tin cover (8)
10 Difficult time to be caught by the dark blue river (6)
12 Student is accepting gold for this animal (5)
13 Mute as Gray's tenor (9)
14 In fine fettle to entertain the merry monarch (3, 2, 1, 6)
18 Awkward in East perhaps to enter in religious community (12)
21 A marigold, strangely nude when in flower (9)
23 The less than all-American girl (5)
24 After work one ingested a narcotic (6)
25 One commonly asleep? Journalist needs to be cured (8)
26 No money, in a way, for Matthew (6)
27 Maybe ten drinker knocked back – could be port (8)

Down

1 Put in the doldrums? Don't panic! (6)
2 False report about balsam (6)
3 Pitcairn Islander was no pagan (9)
4 Reaching game point can be so beneficial (12)
6 Edmund, statesman or murderer? (5)
7 Rocky's got a French sweetheart (8)
8 Small girl's bloomer creates calamity (8)
11 With oil-paint did a ruin in this state (12)
15 Boniface at home we hear with a retainer (9)
16 On a certainty for first place, Peruvian Bark (8)
17 No one upset with row over dish-washer (8)
19 Pip was a palindrome (6)
20 French author composed a duet? About 500 (6)
22 Vasco da Gama's Christmas Day discovery so called (5)

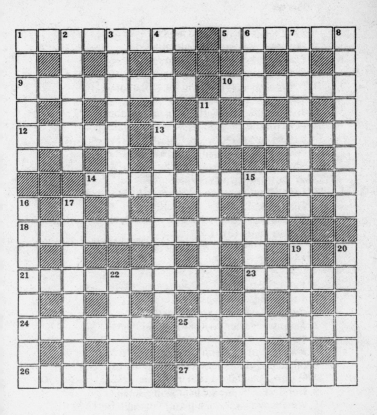

24

Across

1 Give up on account of work (5)
4 Sort of dive some transport drivers hope to avoid (4-5)
9 Cause of ill-feeling in a criminal's wealth (9)
10 One is unusually sound (5)
11 A more oblique means of fixing the joint? (6)
12 One in 400 in Rome (8)
14 Ask too much about the attack (10)
16 Boss seen in a boiled shirt (4)
19 Charged retrospectively – that's bad (4)
20 Are without a host in US party (10)
22 Movie mogul taking half of it could be corrupted (8)
23 In conclusion, 21 does (6)
26 It's obvious there's a split across the island (5)
27 Giant could give Agag a turn (9)
28 Glad of something to brighten us up indeed (9)
29 Tender shark (5)

Down

1 Set a standard weight (9)
2 Arm in plaster if leg is broken? (5)
3 9 points separate couple in scramble (8)
4 Worthless craft (4)
5 A sweet little child. J.R.? Gosh! (7-3)
6 Light the French sort first (6)
7 Foolish about mother, in a manner of speaking (9)
8 Happening to require key on opening (5)
13 For good measure, go in for body-building (4-6)
15 'Time's up!' In exam I produced only part of paper (9)
17 Run down variable gradient to end of line (9)
18 Insect burrowing in level stretch can spoil a lawn (8)
21 Spice provided by one mad Margaret (6)
22 Half of Welsh Nationalists formed by the cloth (5)
24 'We have done but greenly In hugger-mugger to ____ him' (*Hamlet*) (5)
25 Brought up to the sound of common money (4)

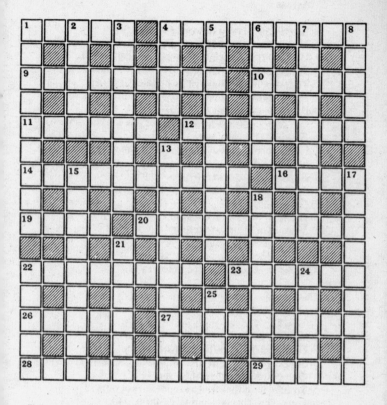

This puzzle, used at the Bristol regional final of the *COLLINS DICTIONARIES* Times Crossword Championship, was solved within 30 minutes by 46 per cent of the finalists.

25

Across

1 Reveller observed returning by ship (9)
6 Miss Aylmer's in bed (5)
9 Hard, in tricky ascent, to impose discipline (7)
10 State of fellow with a following outside Ontario (7)
11 Tell who might carry such a bundle (5)
12 An old railway building accommodating the poor (9)
14 Blossom will perhaps . . . (3)
15 . . . provide food and support for one looking down on Alice. (11)
17 Necessitarian will discourage clergyman without hesitation (11)
19 Rejected Scotsman is a bit eccentric (3)
20 A body's connections in mid-Baltic games organisation (9)
22 Daphne, for one, is cordial (5)
24 Method of selling train that's out of order (7)
26 Type of writer's stress (7)
27 Italian poet relaxed his efforts thus (5)
28 As a rule, this first decision serves (9)

Down

1 Scottish port's sources of heat and light (5)
2 Dignified tinker outside an art gallery (7)
3 Sort of racer, one fit for a skilled mechanic (9)
4 One of 6 across was red for him (11)
5 Strange unauthenticated reports – not ours (3)
6 Hurried to church from stock-farm (5)
7 Main dupe in play (7)
8 Beaten by player it trapped 5 (5-4)
13 It separates strands in Pisa. Kremlin in disarray (11)
14 Leading sportsman's catalogue of successes (9)
16 No way with him, do we infer? (9)
18 Possible man-eater's game with soldiers on ship (7)
19 Anxiety about writer upset by firearm (7)
21 Maxim of abstainer in low surroundings (5)
23 Surrounded like European capital in defeat (5)
25 'The pretty worm of Nilus' (3)

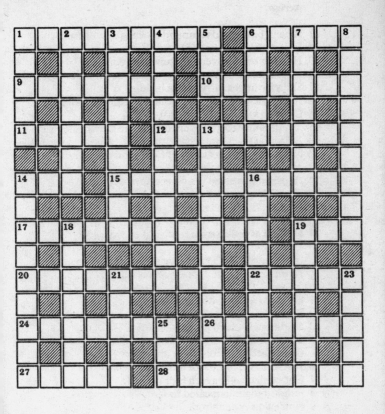

26

Across

1 After a little time flower-girl looks bad-tempered (6)
4 Where to look for pop records? (8)
10 Hill demonstrates dolce far niente . . . (5-4)
11 . . . as does Dr Johnson in his contributions (5)
12 She's in the pink (7)
13 Mere lad appears uncommonly green (7)
14 Dressed for fatigue duty? (5)
15 What some people get up to! (8)
18 Do time-servers get fed up with this? (8)
20 Sticks in a worthless part of London (5)
23 This team is after a win in Sussex (7)
25 Article remodelled in telling fashion (7)
26 Blaze away, say, as pioneers do to make one (5)
27 Being at home, if I marry, is so dull (9)
28 Reade's ready (4, 4)
29 Hat-girl as artist's model (6)

Down

1 One gets fed up with him (8)
2 This soldier should feel at home in the orderly room (7)
3 Might one be seen on a white horse? (4-5)
5 King not subject of the idylls but might describe their
   writer (6, 3, 5)
6 A vine trained in simple form (5)
7 Not quite eighteen inches of rope (7)
8 Show of force, occasionally (6)
9 Noble flower people (5, 3, 6)
16 He certainly has a voice in civic matters (4, 5)
17 Rest play this instrument with variations (8)
19 But it's enjoyed out of doors even in the close season
   (4, 3)
21 All bent on a change of game (7)
22 Drink may so damage one? (6)
24 Frankly this law Henry V disputed (5)

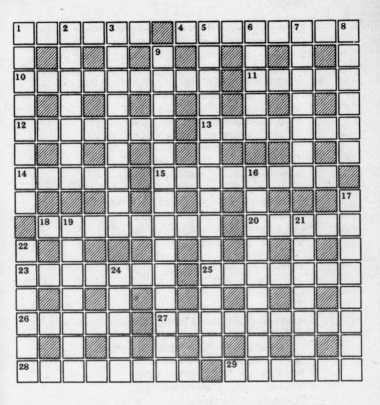

This puzzle, used at the Bristol regional final of the *COLLINS DICTIONARIES Times Crossword Championship*, was solved within 30 minutes by 52 per cent of the finalists.

27

Across

1 Delicately coloured plates broken (6)
5 One holding wheel makes short distance in record at home (8)
9 A soldier leading army to river is a trouble-maker (8)
10 Louisiana to continue to have a sea-water lake (6)
11 Like the Ilano fish in the lock (8)
12 Pass directions around the circuit (6)
13 Jeopardise the aim of the peacemaker (8)
15 Old notes collected (4)
17 Languish in them operatically (4)
19 Pay Miss Love out for drinking parties (8)
20 High standards of thoughts about money (6)
21 Whence came one invasion and whither another (8)
22 Scandinavian, and not Betsey Trotwood's protégé, we hear (6)
23 Dog to compete with below the mill? (4-4)
24 Ruffled dress one approves (8)
25 One elected in the country or dominion (6)

Down

2 Greatly annoying many leaving a place in West Sussex (8)
3 Staggered when man traps fish-eater (8)
4 Young followers, such saints! (6-3)
5 Trade pleases Ann arranging valued possessions (5, 3, 7)
6 Wear for a baby or a swimmer? (7)
7 The Duke appears to thrive on love (8)
8 'Let schoolmasters puzzle their brain, With grammar, and ——, and learning' (Goldsmith) (8)
14 In the forces once, receives cross perhaps (2-7)
15 Flirting, having no head for marriage (8)
16 Made popular Red Dean, perhaps, after start of Easter (8)
17 She of the reptilian allegory (8)
18 Conjurer with rabbit is a man of the theatre (8)
19 One 'full of strange oaths and bearded like the pard' (7)

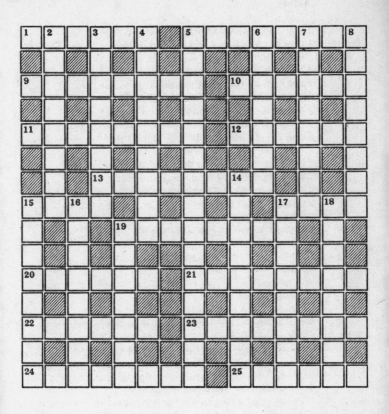

28

Across

1 How boats behave in stormy weather – what a game! (5-3-4)
9 Saki's talking cat in Mull (9)
10 Club to which governor goes for a swim (5)
11 First item for sale on application (6)
12 Bygone test to describe the eclogues (8)
13 One table needs revision, though (6)
15 Zeus, say, adds name to London's show place (8)
18 Bird also pursuing spaniel, one might say (8)
19 Such was Mrs Siddons' muse (6)
21 Half capsized on them – seems to be compensation needed (4-4)
23 Frightful female knocks back no watered rum (6)
26 Abuse in common parlance (5)
27 It includes return of a classic type, a lover (9)
28 Bomb thrower employed in building dugouts? (6, 6)

Down

1 Stroke girl on the knee (7)
2 To put on part with old Jewish bookmaker (5)
3 Instrument redesigned by a choirman (9)
4 Absence of approval for a recess (4)
5 Sound advice to one seeking bargains in canvas (3-5)
6 Peasant wear upsetting to men of degree (5)
7 Flier Jack in army support? (8)
8 A bird to follow Tennyson's gleam (6)
14 Vehicle piled up on another at this game (8)
16 Emissary to the gorgeous East from one once holding it in fee (5, 4)
17 Eccentric and minor artist influenced by . . . (8)
18 . . . Braque, perhaps (measure without direction) (6)
20 Horseman fathered by Ixion (7)
22 Composer makes money in reversal of fashion (5)
24 Conveyance for Ulysses? (5)
25 Between Lincolnshire and Norfolk this used to be hot (4)

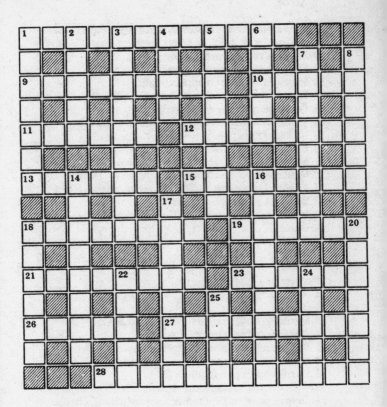

This puzzle, used at the London A regional final of the COLLINS DICTIONARIES Times Crossword Championship, was solved within 30 minutes by 44 per cent of the finalists.

29

Across

1 Agree with conscientious objector in prison, say (8)
5 Seating for choir in All Saints, perhaps (6)
10 Proverbially they act sheepishly (5, 2, 1, 7)
11 She's a Latvian with diamonds! (7)
12 Type of 23 straight from the battle (4, 3)
13 Keep still, by the way, and relatively close (8)
15 About suitable for dockyard job (5)
18 What metal-detectors want to find in abundance,
we hear (5)
20 Detract from Chinese restaurant? (4, 4)
23 Man-at-arms of Scottish breed, maybe (7)
25 Basil dropped in as a matter of good taste (3-4)
26 Painter they call crazy (like this) (15)
27 Sea-cook's side of beef (6)
28 Interfered with spy having key to break signal code (8)

Down

1 Stone is no end of a snob (6)
2 Annoyed girl, having tried awkwardly to embrace her
(9)
3 Moulding outside cover round a kind of bone (7)
4 Daniel is fed up with Old English (5)
6 Seine fisherman going to sea? (7)
7 Franz lost note from Rachel on the way up (5)
8 Proof of spirit power (8)
9 Will this ball, transposed, terminate one's innings? (3-5)
14 Despotism is, to the French, a sort of one-off charity (8)
16 Blow-pipe instrumental in getting something for the pot
(9)
17 Animal which lays eggs by water supply at random (8)
19 Expertise applicable to fiction-writing (7)
21 Letters make it clear to apprentice (7)
22 Call on Tunisian leader to have notes complied with (6)
24 Country has right to mountain range (5)
25 Connected with Cupid (5)

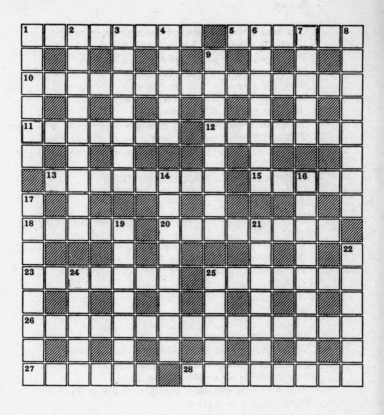

30

Across

1 Gets help that's denied (8)
5 Transport offered to Miss Bell (6)
10 The channel infested with sea-birds? (5)
11 Letter from abroad, not long ago, provides material for this (9)
12 Forgotten, rejected, and so on, in rewritten legend (9)
13 Sorceress left out of the group (5)
14 Complaint I will put before the Head (7)
16 Such variations in meaning heartlessly contrived (6)
19 Young frequenter of the doctor's premises (Fitzgerald) (6)
21 Engineers about to join in retreat by train (7)
23 Deity coming to a bad end in an Indian city (5)
25 Romantic wedding – or goalless draw? (4-5)
27 Stretched thin, the Rev Septimus Harding, if sent back north (4-5)
28 No theatre suffers a setback showing 'Evita' (5)
29 Of which Cowper's hero was a citizen (with credit) (6)
30 Gee! Disco dancing describes the shortest line (8)

Down

1 Titanic, boat grotesque (8)
2 Supporting evil, for instance, friend is outside the law (9)
3 Climbing city street first in fashion (5)
4 What starts things moving? 'Time's up!' (7)
6 An electrical discharge – Sh! that's revolutionary (9)
7 Dismal king in love (5)
8 31 days he gets first from magistrate for g.b.h. (6)
9 Cook's standard of fitness (6)
15 Watch entertainment interrupted by commercial for make-up (3-6)
17 Novel soldiers (3-2-4)
18 He'll repair machine with a bit of care (8)
20 Some graceful marine creature (6)
21 Sir Richard's Nemesis (7)
22 The foreman makes a mistake, right? (6)
24 Note name of material (5)
26 Transport was blue (5)

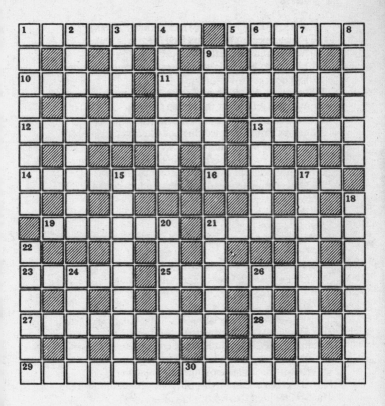

This puzzle, used at the London A regional final of the COLLINS DICTIONARIES Times Crossword Championship, was solved within 30 minutes by 54 per cent of the finalists.

31

Across

1 What it takes to become a churchwarden (8)
5 Flower akin to London Pride? (6)
9 Nothing comes before this (8)
10 Fairy-tale beauty judge apparently changing sides (6)
12 Lift operator of a sort! (5)
13 Light drink? Nonsense! (9)
14 Where Jack is the centre of attraction (7-5)
18 Mad Maria in a hunt for a benevolent man (12)
21 9 days (9)
23 Not what the White Tower was made of (5)
24 Some duty-free, perhaps, one's taken in return journeys (6)
25 Hate a man possibly expressed in a curse (8)
26 Sound as a bell (6)
27 Don't look so closely without a match (8)

Down

1 Quiet watercourses to the mills or folds (6)
2 Such things can be most absorbing (6)
3 Abdicate position as King of the Castle (5, 4)
4 It's a case of being completely taken in (12)
6 They have every prospect of succeeding (5)
7 Strictly speaking, it's what he's expected to be (8)
8 Odd way to estrange a policeman, for instance (8)
11 Rustic merry-making – in a hop-garden? (7, 5)
15 Happy one tops the list up in the Colosseum (9)
16 Solidly built, but a bone-headed lot (8)
17 Antony said it should be made of sterner stuff (8)
19 Stick with present company (6)
20 The way to get around or through the mountains (6)
22 Material appropriate for the barrack-square (5)

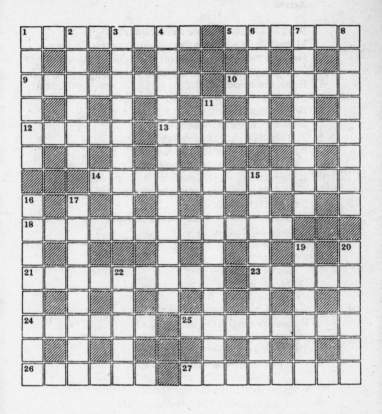

32

Across

1 Born with a duty to give more money (5)
4 Minuscule PCs going after queer characters (9)
9 Girl one Nevada city rejected as religious worker (9)
10 As cold without Latin covering (5)
11 Burden of a good doctor in part of Greater Manchester (6)
12 Wiseacre, pale by dusk (3-5)
14 Lytton's master of murder (6, 4)
16 The way one runs in a bustle (4)
19 Bottom's most fearful wild-fowl (4)
20 Lines heels differently, copies tug-of-war experts (10)
22 It wasn't needed at billiards for making cannons (3-5)
23 Bird produces source of light and its heart (6)
26 Great deal to observe (5)
27 Short treatise, clever and not difficult (9)
28 Continually busy jogging? (2, 3, 4)
29 To rid, wrongly, of a right (5)

Down

1 Rubbish about doctor gets a measure of surprise (9)
2 Pushed forward with assent about two points (5)
3 Drinking seconds – quite happy (8)
4 This rock's no good (4)
5 Warder dances with odd bods (10)
6 '____ thy habit as thy purse can buy' (*Hamlet*) (6)
7 Goes on about a football crowd of vagabonds (9)
8 Newspaper puts ambassador in place (5)
13 In one or two words, what Adam was in original sin (10)
15 Last words in everyday terms (4, 5)
17 Buoyant one right to lie around (9)
18 Like a man in underclothes, all wrong (8)
21 Scowling insect (6)
22 Relish a bit of a blow, love? (5)
24 Indian clerk would make a blunder putting head to tail (5)
25 Dash – jazz is turning up (4)

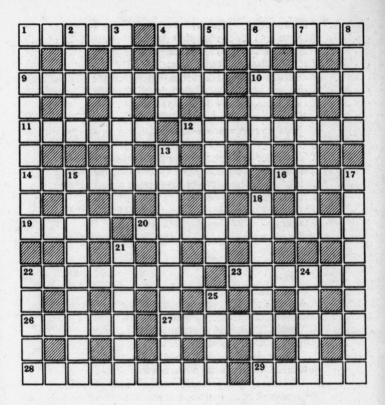

This puzzle, used at the London A regional final of the COLLINS DICTIONARIES Times Crossword Championship, was solved within 30 minutes by 3 per cent of the finalists.

33

Across

1 Chapter (half of it missing) on Miss Pross, for example (8)
9 Better position for a batsman (8)
10 Are magistrates trained in such arts? (4)
11 Harbinger of that which made Isaac reflect (5-7)
13 Silver in Slough? Appearance is illusory (6)
14 Like fire-engines with run of hose (8)
15 New Street's maker of canopies (7)
16 Eldest son heard to question item dealing with inflation (3-4)
20 Chance finding of a small volume, single impression (8)
22 Schools appearing to be for those going places (6)
23 Ask Tapley the sequel to the written enquiry (8-4)
25 In assembly one twice gets the bird (4)
26 In part of play note on keeping still (8)
27 Gave up – what George did about son (8)

Down

2 Parting crack – or rather where it ends (4-4)
3 As plane needs repair, attempts facetious talk (12)
4 Come back again to harvest fruit (8)
5 A moist flower is of this genus (7)
6 Proportionally represented? (6)
7 State service (4)
8 Joined forces working like a horse (6, 2)
12 'Hell is murky' said Lady Macbeth in this scene (5-7)
15 Composed of right and left – quaint arrangement (8)
17 Trains do go out underneath the arch (8)
18 One article in official record gives the petty details (8)
19 Blow struck for beauty (7)
21 Bridge-player not forbidden to call out (6)
24 One test out of a thousand (4)

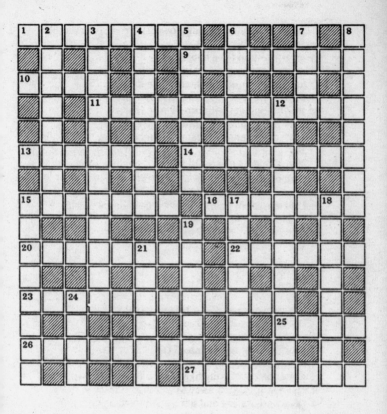

34

Across

1 Provide inspiration for puzzle (6)
4 Victory for William Shakespeare's lord (8)
10 Solicitor working for 'X' (9)
11 Mounting need – no extra money returned (5)
12 Measure 5, perhaps (7)
13 Observantly spot man hiding there (7)
14 Foreign news-agency has nothing on poet (5)
15 Sheep in shelters would exclude ewe, we hear (8)
18 Lanky individual holding runners up (8)
20 Work on ship about to take part in Hunting of the Snark (5)
23 One of the first makers of aprons (3-4)
25 Student team A, on inside and outside (7)
26 Bad temper of people Johnson considered fair (5)
27 Baker Street urchin not obeying rules (9)
28 Use number – note the increase (8)
29 Impudent striker, of course (6)

Down

1 Speak ill of Sheridan's character (8)
2 Good behaviour in police districts, some say (7)
3 Retire from partnership to lower position (5, 4)
5 General manoeuvring men thus? (6, 3, 5)
6 Gradual reduction in girth makes one light (5)
7 Game in which little Dickensian holds bat, perhaps (7)
8 One has no reason to want it (6)
9 How rook moves, but not knight (2, 3, 4, 5)
16 Bet about magistrate taking on belligerent type (9)
17 Fish fashionable poet found under stone (5-3)
19 Speech from the throne (7)
21 Weak points cause ruin of Eblis (7)
22 Duty removed from diamonds (6)
24 Start of Surrey here, perhaps (5)

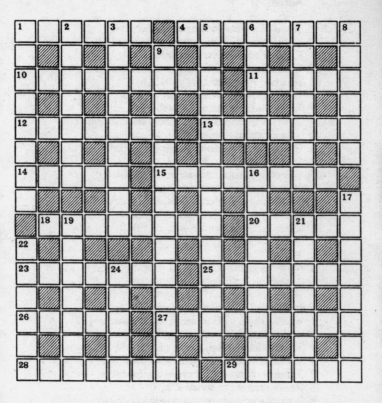

This puzzle, used at the London A regional final of the *COLLINS DICTIONARIES Times Crossword Championship*, was solved within 30 minutes by 18 per cent of the finalists.

35

Across

1 Just a moment, back in half a second (5)
4 Military position moved into a tent (9)
9 Eastern girl's dress ornament (9)
10 Suit; about a month it takes to make (5)
11 Reading-based immunity (7, 2, 6)
12 Extension of a letter, say (6)
14 Want a label in the Strand (8)
17 Articles from abroad, caught in it, abandoned (8)
19 Missing sailors – ten adrift (6)
22 Flora, a leading light (4, 2, 9)
24 Skipper does from half of it (5)
25 Relate to a forward in physical distress (9)
26 One who strives to steer a boat (9)
27 Young trainee acted badly (5)

Down

1 No paying guest has this room above water (4-5)
2 A chap embracing one violently (5)
3 Gentleman John in Nova Scotia (7)
4 In France, have you a note that's sharp? (6)
5 Nine of them will appear as three-quarters (8)
6 Somewhat cloudy, this hypothesis? (7)
7 To be exasperating, I wore mink in the restaurant (9)
8 Vote against holding race; get smart (5)
13 Telling no one, Jack hurried up (9)
15 Rebuilt ten times, a café (9)
16 It holds the blade of a by no means striking poet (8)
18 Inspection of river rising in Cornish resort (4-3)
20 Doctor in eastern island about to be a sword-bearer (7)
21 Lethargy ruined Proust (6)
22 One in bed's getting up, indifferent to pain (5)
23 It's difficult with nothing held in stock (5)

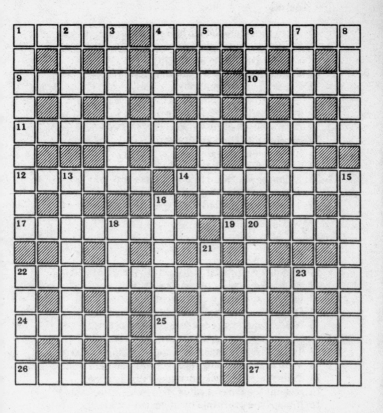

36

Across

1 Unintentional expression of a sinful pride, perhaps (8, 4)
9 Heavyweight to fight heavyweight in South-East? (9)
10 Source of oil, as it happens (5)
11 Vehicle it's illegal to leave in the street (6)
12 Greek king who ruled with a cabinet partly . . . (8)
13 . . . and a couple of chaps like Pythagoras (6)
15 Split found here in region of canine (8)
18 Attack finished weak opponent (4-4)
19 What you might do with hot rod? (6)
21 Exeter man, perhaps, for navy (4, 4)
23 Collector's opening bid for valuable container (6)
26 A danger out east at this time of year (5)
27 A good hand from many MPs . . . (4, 5)
28 . . . where chap seemed in trouble in début (6, 6)

Down

1 Deadlier types such as 10 and 26 (7)
2 Brilliant display from the French (5)
3 Eccentric as odd peer? Bravo! (9)
4 One of several British flowers found in this county (4)
5 Way to stop Henry becoming writer (8)
6 Restrictions for members in these clubs (5)
7 Spiritual guide I had turned up with churchman (8)
8 Main area of Russian and Italian agreement, say (3, 3)
14 Cry for mercy a second before falling in bog (8)
16 Murphy's small contribution to modern technology? (9)
17 Brushed off and polished again (8)
18 President Roosevelt initially bringing in New Deal for vendor (6)
20 Doubly hard to conceal clear changes in Welsh town (7)
22 Where Gilpin meant to dine with a girl (5)
24 Bellows-mender's instrument (5)
25 Make arrangements to get E.T. off earth, say (4)

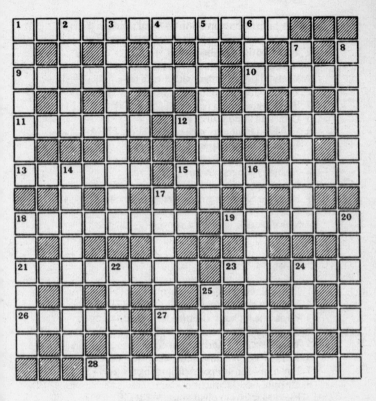

This puzzle, used at the London B regional final of the COLLINS DICTIONARIES Times Crossword Championship, was solved within 30 minutes by 44 per cent of the finalists.

37

Across

1 Press hard to separate the wall of defenders (7)
5 King's visual aid in country of the blind (7)
9 This solution's a wash-out (5)
10 Nine plenty for this solo venture (9)
11 Poetical postscripts of diplomats (6)
12 This recorder said to be heard by one lying on couch (8)
14 Rough sounding? Could be rough if it's white (5)
15 Quartets taking turns to play (9)
18 Full breakfast may mean brown bread (5-4)
20 Bumble's law being one (5)
22 Oil catch freely, being liberal (8)
24 Shutter at shorter range (6)
26 In Greece we hear of this slippery agent (9)
27 Elsinore fop 'spacious in the possession of dirt' (5)
28 Such a girl called one back to Mandalay (7)
29 Sailor, red or white if airborne (7)

Down

1 Display reorganised in Harrow, see (5-4)
2 Many in Bucks town producing fur (7)
3 It may be stored in bottles for safe-opening (9)
4 This cup-bearer sounds very French (4)
5 Weep buckets, perhaps, sadly (10)
6 Russian girl has the makings of a Moon Goddess (5)
7 Lay hands on company following swindle (7)
8 Upright build (5)
13 Field Marshal in eight sounds soft (10)
16 No poltergeist among the spirits here (5-4)
17 It's racial miscegenation to be thus scornful about society (9)
19 Time for some strong ale (7)
21 Take cover from him if you value your life (7)
22 Encoded cable from Moses' spy (5)
23 Branch of A C A S? (5)
25 Painted in Athens, so at variance with a philosopher (4)

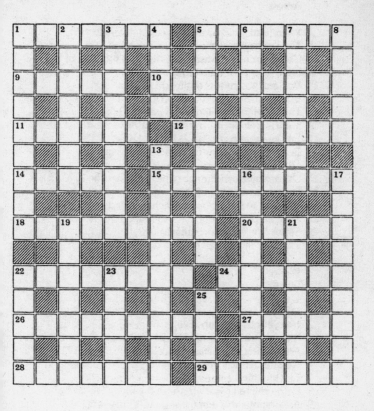

38

Across

1 Strange rite, not all tedious (8)
5 The hound Pashto (6)
10 Oil return has nothing deducted by a member of O P E C (5)
11 Student as a man of the world (9)
12 Bird died in game in church (9)
13 The court of Ferdinand and Isabella? (5)
14 State sources of all rivers in Zambia or North Africa (7)
16 Endlessly collecting fruit (6)
19 In the parsonage, refuge for a wild animal (6)
21 This coat for show? (7)
23 One such bird said to have been soakin' the rich? (5)
25 Late summer's folly (9)
27 Element to be seen in The King's Head (9)
28 Tree as writer (5)
29 Chaucer is hard, like Hamlet (6)
30 Large tin needs repair to make it whole (8)

Down

1 Message for eastern member in public transport (8)
2 Nero libel stirred up revolt (9)
3 It may muffle a vehicle in science fiction (5)
4 Arts master seen about representative colour (7)
6 A mark of one's understanding? (9)
7 Elevate one among many (5)
8 High time to hold it up, that's the idea (6)
9 Arkwright's wood in the state of Minnesota (6)
15 Stops operation by these manual workers (9)
17 Fashionable-sounding ring for Boniface (9)
18 Like him, for example, in the pronominal sense (8)
20 British writer's novel ski-run (6)
21 Retailer to get money out of island (7)
22 Cameraman's supporter makes journey to Cambodians' centre (6)
24 Stick at the wicket (5)
26 Morgan losing his head and his temper (5)

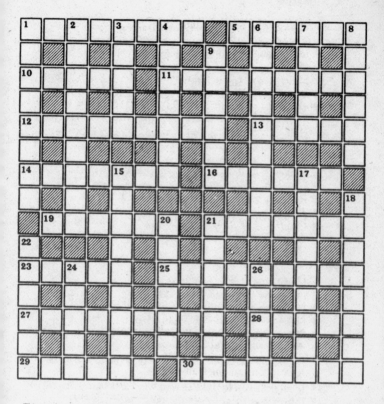

This puzzle, used at the London B regional final of the *COLLINS DICTIONARIES Times Crossword Championship*, was solved within 30 minutes by 45 per cent of the finalists.

39

Across

1 Time to put on gear for beastly training (8)
5 No recent decoration round one theatre (3, 3)
9 A closure arranged in a roundabout way (8)
10 Opera appearing in October only (6)
12 Bit of mirror treated did reflect (5)
13 Space traveller of secondary importance (9)
14 Mocking about the way Colonel was booked (3, 9)
18 Two sorts of seamen like hot cakes (12)
21 Diabolical chief and reprehensible leader (4-5)
23 Words added to text explaining sudden weightlessness? (5)
24 What the doctor ordered for battle injury (6)
25 One of the lengths boxers go to to avoid K O (8)
26 Property – fourth one's found in 22 Street (6)
27 An airy fairy, his Lilian (8)

Down

1 Leave aide gets at length (6)
2 Dark Lady lost lead to Way Out (6)
3 Distasteful money for Canadian song-writer (9)
4 Mechanic to bribe with hundreds of pounds (6, 6)
6 Falsely accuse politician, but not artist (5)
7 Maiden 'bowled' by Piper? (8)
8 Be inclined to meet Conservatives in marginal situation (8)
11 Ideal occasion for setting watch in particular place (8, 4)
15 Inform by repeating points about match, say (9)
16 Prepare for engagement of me, perhaps, to Sarah (8)
17 Missile thrown by good chap on spree (8)
19 Bay horses (6)
20 Like the disheartened navy in our wake (6)
22 Run away from East End prison (5)

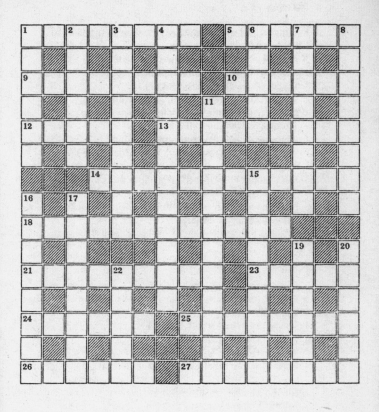

40

Across

1 Produce quiet with a stunning blow on soldier's head (5)
4 I'll get him bad publicity (9)
9 Received several balls before being caught (9)
10 Latter part of 28 said to have signified (5)
11 Change, small change, in root (6)
12 Single us out for a threatening appearance (8)
14 Identical, nevertheless (3, 3, 4)
16 A friend to make much of (4)
19 Fine material from Wimbledon seedings? (4)
20 A man of letters, Leo Tolstoy for instance (4-6)
22 City girl first shows virtue of first president-to-be (8)
23 'Times' indicated by this sort of clue? (6)
26 America, say, backed 28 (5)
27 The family silver, an example of the engraver's skill (4-5)
28 Cure what my attackers get in running water (9)
29 Tobacco for one dissatisfied with original ration (5)

Down

1 Something lacking in America when winter quickly
  follows summer (9)
2 Prince gives a note to the queen (5)
3 Completely wrong direction (8)
4 Superior water colour (4)
5 Bosses heartlessly get two names mixed up (10)
6 Headgear in which one redcap's seen, that's clear (6)
7 Fruit stolen – for use as missiles? (9)
8 Emperor Oates (5)
13 Mayday demands it (10)
15 A crew coming up get beaten outside capital? Just the
  opposite (5-4)
17 Find there's nothing in it (5-4)
18 Try cannabis? That's crazy (8)
21 Mark's grave, perhaps (6)
22 The cellar's clear (5)
24 Animal shown in a book (a picture-book) (5)
25 Issue of magazine turns up (4)

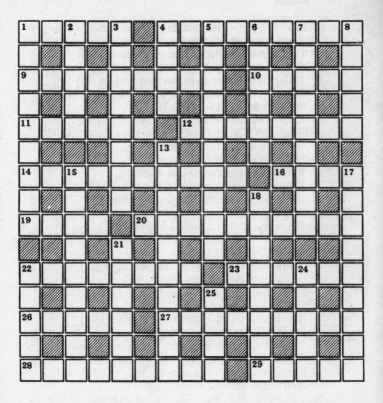

This puzzle, used at the London B regional final of the COLLINS DICTIONARIES
Times Crossword Championship, was solved within 30 minutes by 43 per cent of the finalists.

41

Across

1 Generosity leads me to express wonder (8)
9 American sleeper has some connexion with X (5-3)
10 Puts on party with Poles (4)
11 Biblical 3 action with whips and scorpions (12)
13 More work here – or less, many may hope? (6)
14 The reason, it's said, Henry died of consumption (8)
15 Fighter who left his mark? (7)
16 Continental fair switched to Canada (7)
20 What a blow for the welsher! (8)
22 It's a mug that gets drunk (6)
23 Sort of queer, grisly river beast (4, 8)
25 What's the difference, otherwise? (4)
26 Italian motorway strips initially easy to follow (8)
27 Attending road-trials and getting better? (8)

Down

2 Revolutionary measure with which the bishop
  confronted King Edward (8)
3 Such a code used as a rule in Military Government (12)
4 Hurry up! Don't walk! (8)
5 Run away with fish, following direction (7)
6 I can play with this animal (6)
7 Painful swelling visible in the middle of last year (4)
8 To abandon aircraft is not out of order (8)
12 Climber achieves early fame (7, 5)
15 Sporting rivalry in diamond field (4-4)
17 There's sport before Albert makes it gloomy (8)
18 Big do Ann arranged in Oxfordshire (8)
19 Vessel of some weight in a fight (7)
21 Quotes new style in headgear (6)
24 Amount of cloth needed to cover a girl (4)

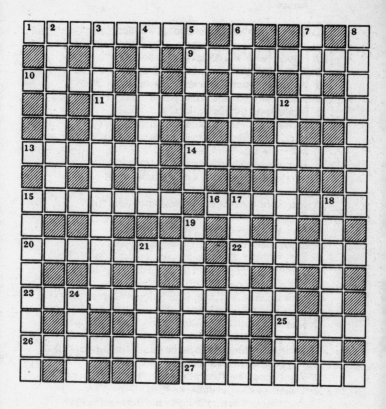

42

Across

1 Old geographer gives nothing to London hospital in return (6)
4 It's the bar of the court, there's no denying (8)
10 Beat artist? (9)
11 Brother (or other relation) of Valentine (5)
12 Stir it into stone (7)
13 Hoffmann's girl shared the fate of Belloc's Matilda (7)
14 Charles has no directions for chopping tree (5)
15 There's nothing right in evil practices – they suck you down (8)
18 Home for a cat-goddess but is taking in bachelors (8)
20 This form of oxygen's a lightweight one (5)
23 Trial, say, you do of Roman military defence (7)
25 Reveal French article, about finished (7)
26 Student owns a place in Tibet (5)
27 No end of money – so cautious a bird! (9)
28 Cry about a mere disaster, e.g. milk spilt here? (8)
29 East German terminus for Belgian destination (6)

Down

1 Fond of company, Italian and Greek islands rise to receive one (8)
2 Of independent means, is he a rip? That's right (7)
3 Crashing a car – habit of Toad and Co. (9)
5 Plant benefiting from Norval's father's frugality (9, 5)
6 Empty-headed, obstinate – what a reputation! (5)
7 Recreation when enjoyed by the older generation (7)
8 Fallen, it yells herein for mercy (6)
9 Remark about railway's first provision for sightseers (11, 3)
16 Press annoyed by German award (4, 5)
17 False beard – yet was shopped (8)
19 Snooty place to steal the limelight? (7)
21 How to get round something, or perhaps above it (7)
22 Such characters are inclined to show stress (6)
24 A foreign member's pacifist suggestion (5)

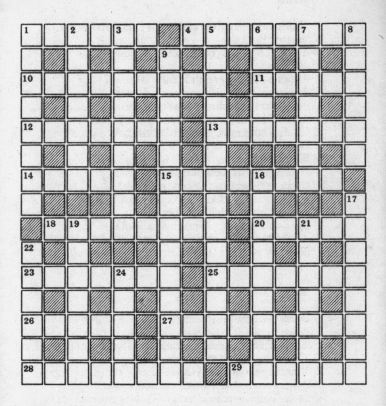

This puzzle, used at the London B regional final of the *COLLINS DICTIONARIES*
Times Crossword Championship, was solved within 43 minutes by 19 per cent of the finalists.

43

 1 Choice of cipher proposed in power politics? (4, 6)
 6 Narcotic drug that was a hanging matter (4)
 9 A lone cub is sadly not mixing with others (10)
10 Measure for fitting, say? (4)
12 Returned in the near-by hillside (4)
13 Black Bess perhaps eating a sort of grain spread (9)
15 I refuse to accept Bird – who is he? (8)
16 A bit of litter near the Hundred Acre Wood (6)
18 Exotic headgear in West End of city (6)
20 Hamlet character perhaps (8)
23 Filling the gap with a curse (9)
24 Province of Greece found in Alaska (4)
26 Eager to behead the king of Israel (4)
27 Possible tie-in with crane to dispose of rubbish (10)
28 Among Jews a gentile returns to this eastern philosophy (4)
29 Adam the first for information leading to Italian gold (10)

Down

 1 Olympian gateway to the East is raised (4)
 2 Proceed, after a fault, with some reticence (7)
 3 Alternatively, treasury considered as having scored (12)
 4 Varieties of meat for a fellow sportsman (4-4)
 5 Tankers able to cope with rough seas (6)
 7 Bones received his visionary prophecies (7)
 8 Senior pupil on river in area of French department (10)
11 It shows pictures of tribe of wise men getting the bird (5, 7)
14 Girl taking in 22 (6, 4)
17 Fixing a job in the shipyard (8)
19 Such yarns excellent if of poor tensile strength? (7)
21 Athlete frequenting bars? (7)
22 Sustenance for this headless man (6)
25 What lame ducks bring up, as we do children (4)

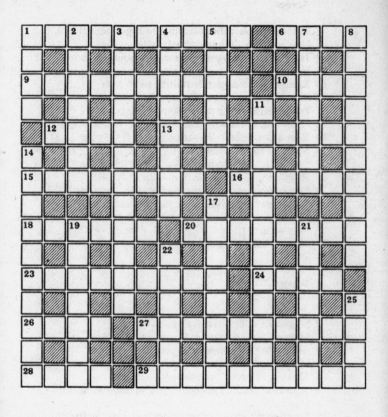

44

Across

1 My sole request about midnight – bring traps round for the old bags (12)
9 Is Egyptian god leading the chosen people? Only one of them (9)
10 Friend I love seen once a year here in Italy (5)
11 Abduct bearer of genetic code during sleep (6)
12 Angry with style in which role is changed (8)
13 Deny West's release from prison (6)
15 Billy has article about garland made from a shrub (8)
18 Material from a fabulous bird in cock-fighting (8)
19 Pioneer of aeronautics, losing at one disastrous swoop (6)
21 Faces of about one thousand beautiful goddesses? (8)
23 Circumnavigating the Pole, the hunter's prayer (6)
26 Sort of suit associated with a caterpillar? (5)
27 Pervasion of cinema with men in disguise (9)
28 Cicely's bed-fellow? (5-7)

Down

1 A bit of a swine, adventuring the last first (7)
2 So ghastly a slur I deny, if not in toto (5)
3 Showing lack of 'give' in Catiline's make-up (9)
4 Set up thus a victim of Polyphemus (4)
5 Drag below the bottom for king-fish catch? (8)
6 This organ has two passages for air (5)
7 Approval thus expressed – a couple of presents, say? (4, 4)
8 Sporting association's intelligence men in the Board of Commerce (6)
14 Spring Month once written by Zola (8)
16 Like what teacher said, old cart in for repair (9)
17 Means of escape studied by the palmist? (8)
18 Sounds like some cheese that's very, very strong (6)
20 Wherein one may see motes – after daylight something larger (7)
22 On the twist, like the resort Noyes recommended (5)
24 Where divine laws broken – by wicked propaganda? (5)
25 The southern gull or small merganser (4)

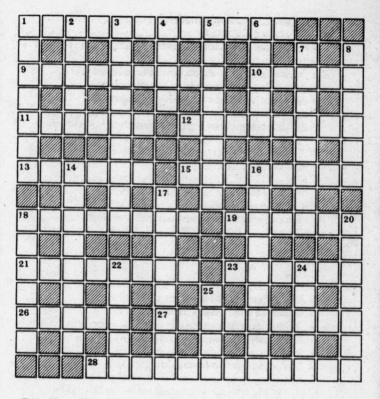

This puzzle, used at the National Final of the *COLLINS DICTIONARIES* Times Crossword Championship, was solved within 30 minutes by 18 of the 20 finalists.

45

Across

1 A horny, as well as a thorny, problem? (7)
5 It's supposed to be put on (7)
9 Meat-cake (meat with egg on in British Rail) (9)
10 Claw the remaining cards (5)
11 A blinking one portrayed in the silver casket (5)
12 This plantation a right bore to stomach! (9)
14 So intimate that some criminals are stupid? (5, 2, 7)
17 One scientist accepts crate ordered for another (14)
21 Made intelligible by former pressman of homely aspect (9)
23 Foster is a shark (5)
24 Curiously overt, Dame Christabel's campaign to be one (5)
25 Name in motor-car accident is Bird (9)
26 Call to get permit? That depends on the head (7)
27 Temporarily debar American writer in South Dakota (7)

Down

1 First-class student had up? What a bloomer! (6)
2 Piece of sugar is hard and heavy (7)
3 A custom he breaks, waxing it? (9)
4 Worsening annoyance (11)
5 It's noted as material for Cockney's 3 (3)
6 In Euripides, a Tyrian wood-god (5)
7 One may be inflamed by such a cocktail (7)
8 Energetic action disturbed Amy's mind (8)
13 Actions in which French artist creates rackets (11)
15 In a tutelary spirit, say, it's skilfully contrived (9)
16 One deputed to watch proceedings weekly (8)
18 A revolutionary means of beaching, for instance (7)
19 Additional identification of vessel in identical surroundings (7)
20 Carefully examined 25 down (6)
22 We hear it said of the ear (5)
25 Spiteful woman jazz enthusiast (3)

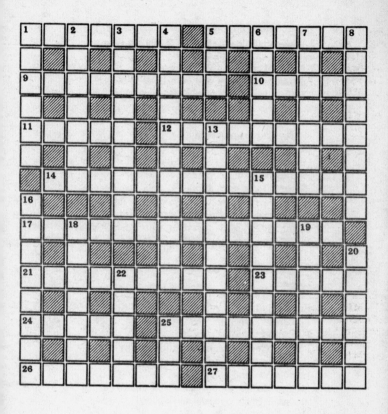

46

Across

1 Painted in water-colours, not by Landseer? (8)
5 Light shoe right for inferior racehorse (6)
10 Place for arms runners (5)
11 Mass trial arranged for flappers (9)
12 Labour activity at grass-roots level? (9)
13 The same urge to be senior member (5)
14 Writer tells how to get Yorktown loser from Cornwall (7)
16 Key operator holds things for us (6)
19 Boatman in Hebrides (6)
21 Complete training, as three-quarters may do (4, 3)
23 Among most, doctors removed anxiety (5)
25 Biggest D-day casualty (4-5)
27 Next man's constructed from rib – enough, is it? (9)
28 19's Rabbit, including one born in this patch (5)
29 Sound quality of British seen in great physician (6)
30 It raises the standing of bell-ringers (8)

Down

1 Equestrian ability possessed by large majority (4, 4)
2 Queen expelling one Roman from place in Egypt (9)
3 Beg for keys (5)
4 Philosopher acting for company, partly (7)
6 Businessmen folding trousers with damaged legs? (4, 5)
7 In river, second bait finally is attracting bites (5)
8 Is, like boxer, coming out of retirement (6)
9 A couple of chaps supposed to help Leo (6)
15 Rack to put case on (9)
17 One involved with cost and no end of money (9)
18 Head's short cut for annual production of scholars? (4, 4)
20 How to train porpoises, for example (6)
21 Losing one's tan a little time afterwards in Sicily? (7)
22 Legislation upset crank found in cabinet (6)
24 Children's author wants decoration round edge (5)
26 Challenge for some athletic Aberdonian? (5)

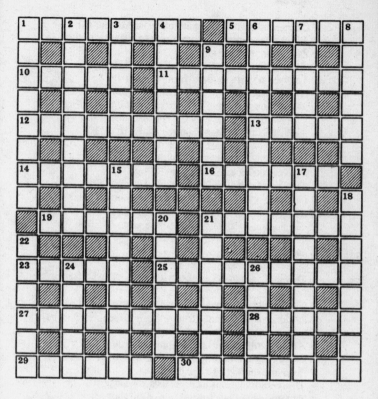

This puzzle, used at the National Final of the COLLINS DICTIONARIES Times
Crossword Championship, was solved within 30 minutes by 16 of the 20 finalists.

47

Across

1 Girl's given credit as an air-traffic controller (8)
9 At home the man has something to pay, it's natural (8)
10 Present in 9 (4)
11 Getting paid for lapse is no different (12)
13 The way papers burn (6)
14 Happening to put two numbers in order (8)
15 Show curiosity about primitive primness (7)
16 Eastern doctor going by old ship put under ban (7)
20 Aquatic creature has to stay back by river (8)
22 Make an anagram of repair (6)
23 Train men to nuclear terminology (12)
25 A river, no? Yes! (4)
26 King's not dead; the business is out in the open (8)
27 Description of what's left is held back in Sir Harry's return (8)

Down

2 One making speeches about gym, or one who performs (8)
3 Cooking she's piped her mashed potato over the meat (9, 3)
4 Grass, not out of an earlier time (8)
5 Kind of energy the family appears to call up (7)
6 Dose with some of Murphy's ice-cream (6)
7 Near the middle (4)
8 There's some point to it; let's change that (8)
12 Appendage of an elderly type of climber (3, 4, 5)
15 Ginger-beer consumed by bird – that's dandy! (8)
17 He's entitled to damage that French ship (8)
18 Flowery plot, one with a shrub (8)
19 Council member set 25 adrift (7)
21 Cut in magnitude, we hear (6)
24 Resentment when I'm turned up very loud (4)

48

Across

1 She received her own thimble as her prize (5)
4 Conveyance from race in which I led before river turn (5-4)
9 To get right loam mixture use Napier's aid to calculation (9)
10 Vanessa perhaps makes mark in Shakespearian role (5)
11 They detest madmen, proverbially heartless (6)
12 Spain's tourist attraction converted into calories (8)
14 Jupiter was one of those known in Barchester (10)
16 Friendly type (4)
19 One who painted Elizabeth topless (4)
20 She was well-oiled at the reception! (4, 6)
22 Indifferent Sheridan character couldn't do this? (8)
23 The way a convict adapts to prison in Germany (6)
26 Furious at loss of opening for plunder (5)
27 Players have strong-box with odd Scottish binding (9)
28 Synthetic material by the Misses Peachum and Waters, say (9)
29 The craft of the Jumblies (5)

Down

1 B R order to get out balance of payments in full (3, 6)
2 Solid gold piece entered in part exchange (5)
3 Jewellery items are removed, doctor, before operations (8)
4 It's up to the old war leader (4)
5 Man of conviction or a trimmer? Paper always about right (4-6)
6 This inventor in turn announces end of play (6)
7 Questioning test in analysis of gin (9)
8 Funny Girl (for Guy) seen around the river (5)
13 He prevents enjoyment of booty left on board (5-5)
15 One lent its name to the Arrow-maker's daughter (9)
17 Run down, dear, and get in somehow (9)
18 Lover is married, I emphasise (8)
21 Put forward tricky legal point (6)
22 Press Charles the First to meet the parliamentarian (5)

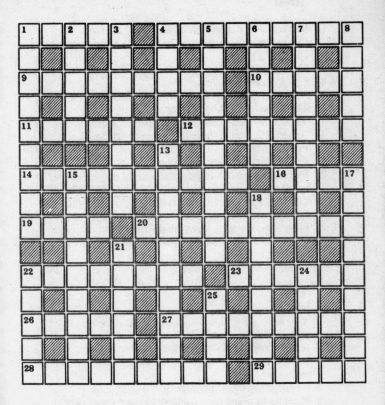

This puzzle, used at the National Final of the COLLINS DICTIONARIES Times Crossword Championship, was solved within 30 minutes by all the 20 finalists.

24 Turner has health ruined by hospital omission (5)
25 '. . . from cliff and ____ The horns of Elfland' (Tennyson) (4)

49

Across

1 Premier going round the circle in this tube (5)
4 Demonstrates round about in Conservative parts outside London (9)
9 Nine great characters from Orange (9)
10 Last in in the river (5)
11 Sharp noise is true maybe in strange tune by Tchaikovsky? (10, 5)
12 Take it the animal heard you and me (6)
14 Reading undergraduates doing this? (8)
17 Former unruly rioter is outside (8)
19 Let Labour see content of money-market (6)
22 Royal bodyguard's regimentals meant one less to be changed (9-2-4)
24 Composer rejects Cockney's comment on weather (5)
25 Hurried back using the oars, reducing the gap thus (9)
26 Is a Hanoverian king indeed disputed? (9)
27 Girl takes Poles round America (5)

Down

1 Monarch and a poet, tent-makers (9)
2 You French reciprocate about a point of principle (5)
3 Proposition for article on Rome riots (7)
4 Hamlet's most important part (6)
5 Takes tea perhaps during parts of game, but not to this extent (8)
6 Steeped in Origin of Fabianism (second-hand) (7)
7 Nicol and I break into a vehicle of the council (9)
8 Note – a great day to do your present job (5)
13 Weekend saints, perhaps? Quite the opposite (9)
15 Lubricator for an egg? Sure crazy! (6-3)
16 Start company to take many people to church (8)
18 Very rich like Chesterton's drunkard (7)
20 Almost 1 across possibly on second choices (7)
21 Caught in tin – a colour (6)
22 The game's up! Edward's confined to school (5)
23 Wrecks one in races (5)

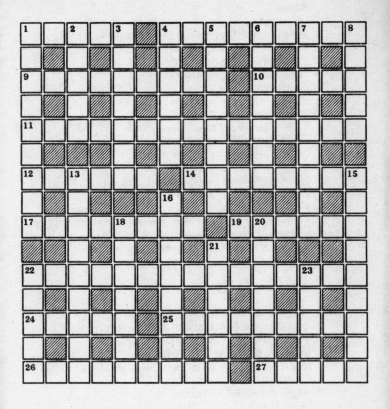

Across

1 The powers that be say I'm in the engineers (6)
4 Riverside fight setting a high tone (8)
10 Suitor with scheme to embrace one pet (9)
11 Loose relative seen topless (5)
12 Advantage point after first of balls, if returned into net (7)
13 Child presented to a princess (7)
14 River in South of France flowing backwards (5)
15 Free ball produces clearance (8)
18 Elegant newcomer to broadcasting (8)
20 Cesario's building at Olivia's gate? (5)
23 Soldiers ordered to carry gear (7)
25 Bring up point repeatedly about money (7)
26 Run over (5)
27 Befuddle and confuse Irene a bit (9)
28 Of different shades of meaning (8)
29 Accomplished by a doctor, there's nothing to it (6)

Down

1 About to open Plato's work (8)
2 Reading out a description of leather (7)
3 Show love in a public declaration (9)
5 In Berlin, so long as we feud in here, it'll be turbulent (3, 11)
6 Material's difficult to hear (5)
7 Huge, and sort of acid (7)
8 I ponder aloud, for no return (3-3)
9 Visitor's limits in Canadian city, below the station (8, 6)
16 Equipped with a sort of crude coat (9)
17 One's concern being the yield, perhaps (8)
19 Part of service record is let out (7)
21 A bold front supplies support against trouble (7)
22 Religious leader marries Jack to Elizabeth (6)
24 Stand by for a pound, say, for instance (5)

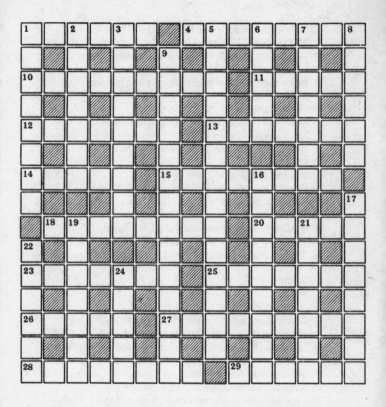

*This puzzle, used at the National Final of the COLLINS DICTIONARIES Times
Crossword Championship, was solved within 30 minutes by 17 of the 20 finalists.*

51

Across

1 Was it form-filling that sent him mad? (5, 4)
6 But grandma was no breaker of tables (5)
9 Act revised to include nude entertainment (7)
10 Young devil pops in to beat one of the drums (7)
11 What a new school needs to get to be progressive? (5)
12 In Crimean mix-up I'm exceedingly gloomy (9)
14 A little sun fish (3)
15 Rainbow trout so amused to be thus made monochrome? (7, 4)
17 Critic of Wordsworth as sonneteer seen in the Abbey? (5, 6)
19 Flier in a cat-fight (3)
20 Step in, in tricky event, without hesitation (9)
22 One's returned in state – hence Columbus (5)
24 Bordered on being an object of ridicule to newsman (7)
26 Sounds like landlord's table inside the ship (7)
27 Pass on and leave a holy man in California (5)
28 Temperamental Muppet was so obstinate! (9)

Down

1 Black stone home whither perhaps 100 came (5)
2 Be right in the red if this describes your cheques (7)
3 Historian's ordered out among miracle-play villains (9)
4 Met blow-out as one might describe it? (11)
5 Amphibian's decapitated – not right (3)
6 Married French girl-friend so-called? (5)
7 Hail perhaps in Westminster district in this tongue (7)
8 Sail hoisted when slow bowler captures a Kent opener (9)
13 Lead-swinging art master unwilling to leave? (11)
14 First singer in tears if more than one such rebuke (9)
16 Terribly glib, I ride in a sort of airship (9)
18 What fans do in French – so English! (7)
19 Foreign leader away from the coast in the country (7)
21 A riot that's out of proportion (5)
23 Some had dedicated what is put on (5)
25 A pickpocket – one that's fairly lucky! (3)

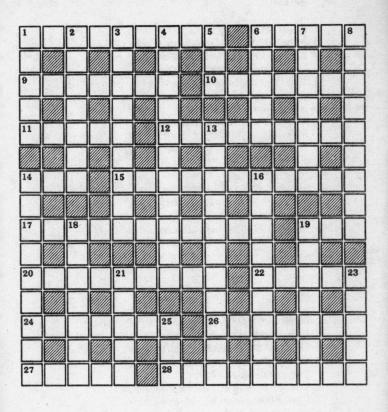

52

Across

1 Endlessly deceiving Poe's detective (5)
4 Name of joiner in 'Berry & Co.' (9)
9 Courses in confectionery-making (9)
10 Unfinished book shelf (5)
11 Was this creature a dissenter? (6)
12 Altering the whole arrangement (8)
14 Sailor has repeated success on board (6, 4)
16 The course in which we came to grief (4)
19 Mary's brother's skipper, perhaps (4)
20 Need Ulster trip appear dull? (4-6)
22 Prediction by old government department about players (8)
23 Measure of drink that's supplied by 24's attendant (6)
26 Get young Val converted in church (5)
27 Writer Jack's no dull boy (9)
28 Late border music (4, 5)
29 Finished letter written to theologian about sweetheart (5)

Down

1 Unemployment act? (9)
2 Like things including many excuses (5)
3 Observing breakdown of refrigerator? (8)
4 Some cottage, doubtless old (4)
5 Top gambling game (3-3-4)
6 Feature of rougher sea – and smoother (6)
7 Sort of trade word for the weed (9)
8 Make one's abode at Land's End – fancy that! (5)
13 Minister seen in theatre – singular (10)
15 Burney's novel about rising artist and body of intriguers (9)
17 Introduced tense Essex and Derbyshire openers (9)
18 Consider putting spirit in tea perhaps (8)
21 Outcry caused by McRae's replacement (6)
22 Confronted with various notes (5)
24 Local VIP at end of trail on road to Scotland (5)
25 Stroke gets a run (4)

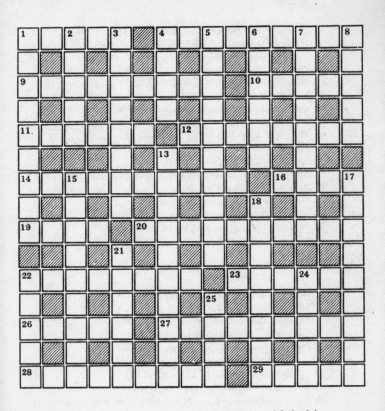

This puzzle, used as a tie-breaker at the Glasgow and Bristol regional finals of the COLLINS DICTIONARIES Times Crossword Championship, was solved on each occasion in under 8 minutes.

53

Across

1 Wine for medical profession, colloquially speaking (5)
4 Diamond could be such a valuable resource (5, 4)
9 View of countryman canvassed, so to speak (9)
10 Lowest point in production a director conceals (5)
11 Blue-stocking in place of queen? (5)
12 Low-budget hit, this one (9)
13 Antiquated weapon for Great War soldier (3, 4)
15 Sort of library which may provide a bit of interest? (7)
18 Bird with heavenly body Flanagan embraced (7)
20 Recorded snub (3, 4)
21 Large bird's fair feature (3, 6)
23 Show repugnance concerning apocryphal idol (5)
25 Serious but not acute (5)
26 By no means fit, being misshapen? (3, 2, 4)
27 West Indian players have strong all-rounder (5, 4)
28 Athenian who produces metal in any case (5)

Down

1 Explosive device making philosopher's fortune? (5, 4)
2 Ball – but it could be square (5)
3 Fellow-actor one follows about the country (5, 4)
4 Greeting Tory leader with reprimand (7)
5 Not even Leo is such a shareholder (7)
6 Attractive type, secure in high position . . . (3-2)
7 . . . and opposed to no movement (9)
8 100-yard burst for Austen's hero (5)
14 Letters from Danes I get (in the post but not yet arrived) (9)
16 Fisherman's return? (3, 6)
17 Players' opponents once, including pair from Verona? (9)
19 Document awarded to one old map-maker (7)
20 Silver, for instance, and old copper plundered (7)
21 Vehicle holds up progress? Not true (5)
22 Indeed, all the odd bits are perfect (5)
24 Perfection of Joyce's character (5)

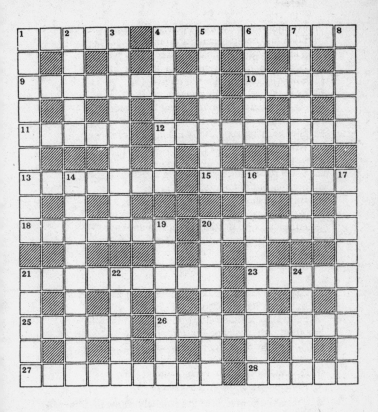

54

Across

1 Could be posh sounding lot of fertiliser (9)
6 Plain place in which evil was so dominant (5)
9 Refuse to make a scathing comment (7)
10 Dress case to shift (7)
11 Submit a return (5)
12 Scrambler for a helicopter (3-6)
13 Correction one printed without fear (8)
15 Cut price bargain (4)
19 One of Rosencrantz's young hawks (4)
20 Took a curve on the Underground with rash intent (4-4)
23 Camelford replanned as protected area for shooting (4-5)
24 It secures seat by curious right (5)
26 Unhappy men in the East get no recall (7)
27 Being green I turn dizzy with this (7)
28 Assume one's in the mail (5)
29 Embankment, part of third day's programme in the beginning (9)

Down

1 Telecommunications policy? (5-4)
2 Man in Spain loses hard game (5)
3 Kneel in prayer here for endlessly deformed Euripides (4-4)
4 Muscular Oldham follower (8)
5 Take on to enter into conflict (6)
6 It lasts the course, like the man who came to dinner (6)
7 Emergent woman (9)
8 One taking part in the social or the kitchen whirl (5)
14 They determine the ground to be covered by conveyances (9)
16 Football field with one man threatening two with a haymaker (9)
17 Roger says this works (8)
18 One of the short list on the governing body (8)
21 Compensation where film actors aren't performing? (6)
22 Vessel for a service in church (6)

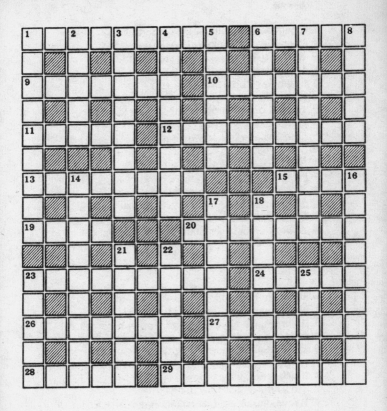

23 Contraction familiar to a prolific writer? (5)
25 Money one might charge in a wildlife park? (5)

55

Across

1 Cancel immediately, we hear (5, 3)
5 Gets worn in the first of several strikes (6)
10 Waits for production of this book (1, 9, 5)
11 Such edible delight (7)
12 I am quietly learning to beg (7)
13 Giving speech, don't start being inaudible (8)
15 The long, not the Spanish, leather (5)
18 Island in which a river flowed (5)
20 Conquistador's not finished holding surgeon in warship (8)
23 Pools of it around in aircraft (7)
25 Promising youngster sated with Ruritania? (7)
26 Uninvolved as car crashes in the vicinity of Victoria (9, 6)
27 Did a dance having brought in the catch (6)
28 Bowler, for instance, had to agree to differ (8)

Down

1 Successfully breaking the law can result in it (6)
2 He succeeds in transmuting their gold (9)
3 Building uninsured if I cease to provide cover for it (7)
4 Sell for double (5)
6 Here's the main part of 22 (7)
7 Give up oriental game to leading pro (5)
8 Roughly speaking what greengrocers do with a cloth border? (8)
9 To avoid work eat abroad (about £1) (8)
14 Cutting in is vice to be punished (8)
16 Stone might be so obsolete (3-2-4)
17 Trample on a piece of cake (4-4)
19 Offensive order given during a row (7)
21 Former spouse sat in the open (7)
22 It's powerless to fly (6)
24 Colour can turn up for instance (5)
25 Husky, they say, is a beast of burden (5)

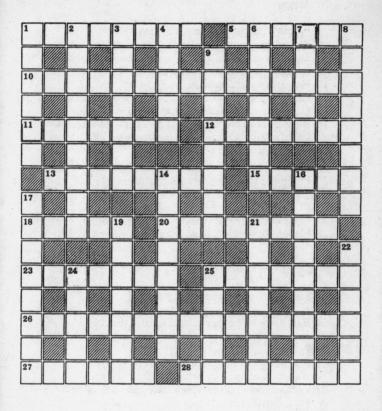

Across

1 Woollen headgear a danger in plant (8)
5 Poured insults on America in retirement (6)
9 Sort of bodily harm alleged against man in charge (8)
10 Ballerina deserted by a physiologist (6)
12 Revolver for chopper (5)
13 Like U S Defense H Q getting 20 per cent increase? (9)
14 Go in terror at brutal treatment of questionmaster (12)
18 Rescue about fifty clubs from harsh employers (5-7)
21 Lame radio operators go to town in Herts (9)
23 Oriental looks like a Scotsman (5)
24 With learned cleric brought in man of action is seen to tremble (6)
25 Offering effective consumer resistance (8)
26 Swift flying resort of gullible speculators (6)
27 Transport to excavate an early Welsh urban settlement? (8)

Down

1 Poet upset at evidence of carnage (6)
2 Half Isle of Man's turnover yet to be worked out (6)
3 Paul takes bearing on church in Bow (9)
4 Isolated part of state dependent on Falklands (5, 7)
6 Pot-plant gets sound report (5)
7 The quality of Athenian wit? (8)
8 Eamon read out a farewell utterance in it (2, 6)
11 Further two states join New Zealand – a show of eccentricity (12)
15 Country to east in French department is flower-bedecked (9)
16 Deal with shop producing heavenly plant hybrid (8)
17 Brought to a higher degree of readiness for the race? (6, 2)
19 Container for what Christopher shot? (6)
20 Fashionable bird? Shut up! (6)
22 River as council site (5)

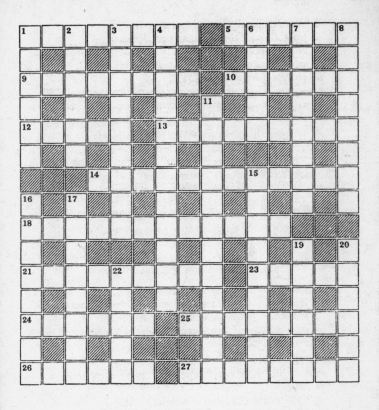

57

1 Thing which in Latin would be in the 9 (6)
5 Bridge partners retrieved bloomer of Saki's
  Gabriel-Ernest (8)
9 The Dreyfus Case, for Zola? (10)
10 Classic wear put by Sara in a trunk (4)
11 Dick's repeatedly said to be such a beast (8)
12 Monster spelling the end of Christian's advance (6)
13 Had made a night, say, of this festive occasion (4)
15 Weapon for torturing – it's a crime, almost (8)
18 Team's mouthpiece seen in air or snow manoeuvre (4-4)
19 Robert appears to strip (4)
21 Did an alleged assassin do without laws in retrospect?
  (6)
23 This laboratory not needed before Babel (8)
25 Mineral revealed by a sound prophet (4)
26 Sea creature to enrich mode with variations (10)
27 A bishop's throne without indication of the new
  recipient (8)
28 Turf study shows it's very wet (6)

Down

2 Lack of transport upset Francis (5)
3 Count's revised menu was in Latin, note (9)
4 Hatter's repository for a dormouse? (6)
5 Wet, deep and churlish perhaps describes a hypocrite
  (6, 9)
6 Speeches of Gladstone, inebriated, verbose (Disraeli)
  (8)
7 First element associated with diamonds (or ice) (5)
8 Member's not in time to do housework (9)
14 Easy position? (9)
16 I am beaten? Shut up! (9)
17 Leg bound to be broken by this weapon (8)
20 An article like 'Fruit' (6)
22 Family of Cremona beloved by Romans (5)
24 Shrub could be no end of 12 (5)

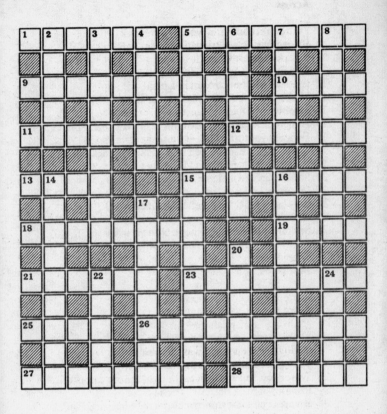

58

Across

1 Do keep crow to replace this bird (10)
6 Bound to be a slight advantage (4)
10 The rises awaited by Micawber? (7)
11 Trying to sink, dispatching shot thus? (7)
12 Provide another sort of bridge (9)
13 Man's name for river, sacred one (5)
14 Symbol you need to know (5)
15 Brush-off repels Sidney introducing himself to girl (9)
17 Deal roughly with chap holding North hand (9)
20 Superficial brilliance of county side's opener (5)
21 Relaxation allowed at University (3-2)
23 Such an estate makes payment easy (3, 6)
25 Observe a measure of power, reversing this vehicle (7)
26 Like rag-and-bone firm? By no means (7)
27 Occupant of larger nest (4)
28 Meddle half-heartedly with 22 – this could result (10)

Down

1 Proceeded in crooked fashion to cause injury (5)
2 Blunt confirmation of 15 (9)
3 Motorists' fluffy cats best on floor? (7, 7)
4 Share best parts with daughter in The Big Apple (7)
5 22 no longer involved in paperwork? (7)
7 Recognised procedure that can be boring (5)
8 They must be broken when letting the clutch out (9)
9 Firearm driving Falstaff's friend from lair (8-6)
14 Boy gets pass for this special sort of film (4-5)
16 By implication hide the rest of this excellent specimen? (4-5)
18 Backs party, in case (7)
19 Get artist a seat for the play (7)
22 Aim of series is to instruct (5)
24 Cheat in friendly alien country (5)

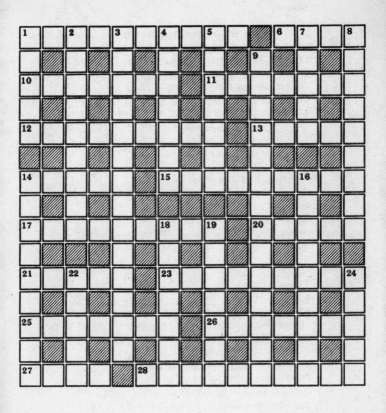

Across

1 A scrupulous person, and a persistent one, about money (8)
9 Point to Greek letter with curve in the inscription (8)
10 Right position of course – north (4)
11 Man of theatre has varied views (5-7)
13 Looks for a way up, say? (6)
14 It is to one law-maker lawful, that goes without saying (8)
15 Unusual issue of notes (7)
16 Scheme includes also some soldiers (7)
20 Use some silk in one's suit? (8)
22 Henry IV's character very weak (6)
23 Poetic hamlet in general, with church and spreading trees (12)
25 In court, witness appears a fool? (4)
26 Space traveller is given a hormone, perhaps (8)
27 Sadness beginning during this sort of spree? (8)

Down

2 Persevering type is about satisfied with verse (8)
3 Argument against writing to one concerning a war-time measure (12)
4 One allowed to make bargains? (8)
5 Day-dreaming parson on the lake (7)
6 Mulled and spiced wine on board? (6)
7 Some uppish gunners in training (4)
8 He was associated with the cabinet in Pitt's day (8)
12 A friend at the gathering appears timorous (5-7)
15 Message gives border rent rise (8)
17 Duration of seven 24 on the world stage (8)
18 Offering an obol – it appears odd (8)
19 Tales traditionally down to earth? (7)
21 At which tramps may ride (6)
24 Apostolic performances (4)

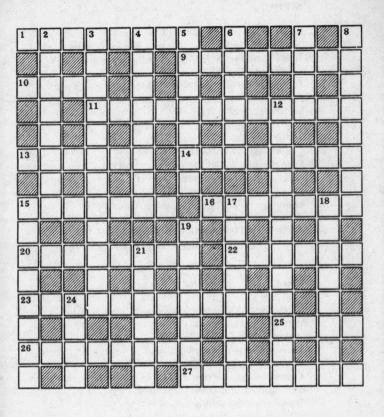

60

Across

1 One had a wife hit the nail on the head (6)
4 A universal international system in 9 fit for artisans (8)
10 Now, some say, a new name for things intuitively perceived (7)
11 Cab for Lady Griddlebone's wooer after losing game (7)
12 After drink 'e takes the trail, withered but hanging on (10)
13 Self-announced pirate? (4)
15 Like the energy one is still lacking (7)
17 No small 11 caused this great disaster (7)
19 Paul invested therewith? (7)
21 Like big guns led by King Cole to find her (7)
23 So address the Great Man 'tuan' continuously (4)
24 Savage's beloved (if second-best) things (6, 4)
27 Hits object back that's reeking noxiously (7)
28 Honor est a Nilo, anagrammatically won here (7)
29 Oolite found by line, say, and weight (8)
30 Dreaded wolf – one runs by marsh and river (6)

Down

1 Sandi booked as successful draughts player (4-5)
2 This star creates run on extraterrestrial materials (7)
3 O that artist – so dated! (10)
5 Oriental spirit captured in a neat arrangement of these marbles (9)
6 Deranged running thus? But nothing wrong with me (4)
7 Fair-visaged, one namesake of this king? (7)
8 Many a goldfish in this castle (5)
9 Whence justice is dispensed (or money, we hear?) (4)
14 It records heights of poet's Tosca version (10)
16 Old king caught Joshua's father craftily holding daggers (9)
18 Mad character in church, right talkative bird (9)
20 Richard had parts to play in Wiltshire (7)
22 Fast horse for sale's sound (7)
23 Lucia's operatic alias – right guardian of wisdom's fountain (5)
25 Reverse of healthy place for David's victim (4)
26 Neglect a thousand-to-one possibility (4)

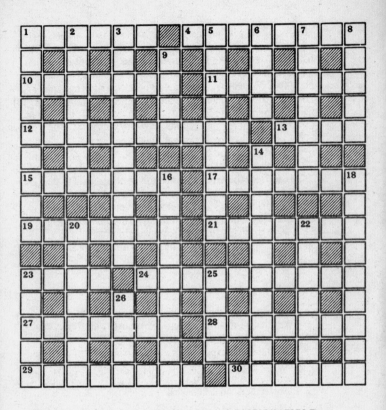

60

This was the Eliminator Puzzle in the 1983 *COLLINS DICTIONARIES* Times
Crossword Championship mentioned in the Foreword.

The Solutions

No. 1

ACROSS – 1, Begat; 4, Applejack; 9, Odourless; 10, Patna; 11, Yellow; 12, Imprimis; 14, Robustness; 16, Atom; 19, Pier; 20, Copernicus; 22, Attitude; 23, Treble; 26, Mania; 27, Rectangle; 28, Discerned; 29, Homer.

DOWN – 1, Booby-trap; 2, Growl; 3, Tarboosh; 4, Amen; 5, Past master; 6, Empire; 7, Automatic; 8, Keats; 13, Any old iron; 15, Beestings; 17, Musketeer; 18, Encroach; 21, Strake; 22, Armed; 24, Begum; 25, Iced.

No. 2

ACROSS – 1, Accept; 4, Two by two; 10, Admiral; 11, Yorkers; 12, Travancore; 13, Emil; 15, Satiric; 17, De facto; 19, Aerosol; 21, Enclose; 23, Gang; 24, Cole Porter; 27, Angelus; 28, Pianola; 29, Tuesdays; 30, Portly.

DOWN – 1, Anastasia; 2, Compact; 3, Permafrost; 5, Weybridge; 6, Bari; 7, Thermic; 8, Ousel; 9, Bloc; 14, Aficionado; 16, Callously; 18, Oven-ready; 20, Renegue; 22, Outpost; 23, Grant; 25, Espy; 26, Olid.

No. 3

ACROSS – 1, Outbids; 5, Ruffian; 9, Chain; 10, Animation; 11, Assertion; 12, Swore; 13, Drove; 15, Niggardly; 18, Bolstered; 19, Fleet; 21, Split; 23, Brassière; 25, Face-cloth; 26, Eliot; 27, Lamprey; 28, Riposte.

DOWN – 1, Orchard; 2, Toadstool; 3, Inner; 4, Stationer; 5, Reign; 6, Flagstaff; 7, Inigo; 8, Nunnery; 14, Estate car; 16, Godfather; 17, Dietetics; 18, Bashful; 20, Theatre; 22, Locum; 23, Booty; 24, Sleep.

No. 4

ACROSS – 1, Face-ache; 5, Staple; 10, Abash; 11, Square leg; 12, Pikestaff; 13, Sheet; 14, Reached; 16, Railed; 19, Reward; 21, Pretext; 23, Crass; 25, Calenture; 27, Temporise; 28, Opium; 29, Hedger; 30, Assigned.

DOWN – 1, Flappers; 2, Crankcase; 3, Athos; 4, Husband; 6, Turnstile; 7, Pulse; 8, Eights; 9, Buffer; 15, Headstone; 17, Execution; 18, Streamed; 20, Dacoit; 21, Palmers; 22, Scotch; 24, Armed; 26, Naomi.

No. 5

ACROSS – 1, Jackanapes; 6, Barb; 9, Denudation; 10, Shah; 12, Near; 13, Truncheon; 15, Solitude; 16, Quench; 18, Relent; 20, Homespun; 23, Labourers; 24, Core; 26, Gnat; 27, Permanence; 28, Rays; 29, Door-keeper.

DOWN – 1, Jade; 2, Conceal; 3, Adder's tongue; 4, Attitude; 5, Exodus; 7, Achaean; 8, Behindhand; 11, Acquiescence; 14, Astrologer; 17, Gossamer; 19, Library; 21, Parsnip; 22, Hereto; 25, Weir.

No. 6

ACROSS – 1, Parish priest; 9, Reinforce; 10, Igloo; 11, Greats; 12, Wide open; 13, Europa; 15, Clambake; 18, Chain-saw; 19, Orchis; 21, Overnice; 23, Cicada; 26, Cutis; 27, Paramount; 28, Frankenstein.

DOWN – 1, Pirogue; 2, Raise; 3, Safety-pin; 4, Part; 5, Ice-field; 6, Swine; 7, Slapdash; 8, Bounce; 14, Reagents; 16, Martinmas; 17, Saucepan; 18, Choice; 20, Spartan; 22, Noser; 24, Acute; 25, Brie.

No. 7

ACROSS – 1, Firefly; 5, Musical; 9, Elfin; 10, Liquorice; 11, Martyr; 12, Mistakes; 14, Steer; 15, Alligator; 18, Nattering; 20, Light; 22, Bestride; 24, Legion; 26, Tricolour; 27, Radii; 28, Durable; 29, Elderly.

DOWN – 1, Freemason; 2, Referee; 3, Fancy-free; 4, Yelp; 5, Maquillage; 6, Scout; 7, Cricket; 8, Leeks; 13, Palindrome; 16, Goldenrod; 17, Rotundity; 19, Tastier; 21, Guilder; 22, Bated; 23, Rhomb; 25, Tree.

No. 8

ACROSS – 1, Barge; 4, Charlatan; 9, Tenacious; 10, Twain; 11, Sleepy; 12, Dialysis; 14, Empedocles; 16, Moss; 19, Arno; 20, Inoculated; 22, Shamrock; 23, Burgee; 26, Ovolo; 27, Armadillo; 28, Conductor; 29, Rider.

DOWN – 1, Bathsheba; 2, Ranee; 3, Escapade; 4, Cook; 5, Abstinence; 6, Little; 7, Transport; 8, Nones; 13, Iconoclast; 15, Pantaloon; 17, Sedgemoor; 18, Flounder; 21, Ormolu; 22, Stoic; 24, Gelid; 25, Omar.

No. 9

ACROSS – 1, Paragon; 5, Popular; 9, Alban; 10, Waistcoat; 11, Exuberant; 12, Royal; 13, On dit; 15, Touchwood; 18, Bedspread; 19, Macho; 21, Colon; 23, Irregular; 25, Home-ruler; 26, Alarm; 27, Synonym; 28, Discern.

DOWN – 1, Placebo; 2, Rebounded; 3, Genre; 4, Newcastle; 5, Point; 6, Petersham; 7, Loony; 8, Rattled; 14, Tip and run; 16, Underbred; 17, Oscillate; 18, Bacchus; 20, Oarsman; 22, Lemon; 23, Islam; 24, Glass.

No. 10

ACROSS – 1, Scampi; 4, Commuter; 10, Imperfect; 11, Grail; 12, Another; 13, Fatigue; 14, Lie in; 15, Nihilist; 18, Majestic; 20, Brace; 23, Humdrum; 25, Martini; 26, Range; 27, Spoonbill; 28, Backside; 29, Shaggy.

DOWN – 1, Suitable; 2, Approve; 3, Perchance; 5, Out of the common; 6, Might; 7, Tear-gas; 8, Roller; 9, We are not amused; 16, Labyrinth; 17, Menially; 19, Almanac; 21, Abiding; 22, Cherub; 24, Reefs.

No. 11

ACROSS – 1, Pearl-diver; 9, Uganda; 10, Herdsman; 11, Take heed; 12, Isle; 13, Readjusted; 15, Dictate; 17, Gilbert; 20, Liquescent; 21, Hals; 23, Cressida; 25, Proposal; 26, Tattle; 27, Sneak-thief.

DOWN – 2, Erebus; 3, Redolent; 4, Democritus; 5, Ventral; 6, Ruck; 7, Unsettle; 8, Candidates; 12, Indelicate; 14, Joint-stock; 16, Coquette; 18, Behemoth; 19, Relapse; 22, Legate; 24, Ides.

No. 12

ACROSS – 1, Dressing down; 9, Waste-pipe; 10, Drake; 11, Galore; 12, Although; 13, Ranker; 15, Minehead; 18, Obtusely; 19, Vessel; 21, Doorpost; 23, Aghast; 26, Inept; 27, Ghost-like; 28, Hypnotically.

DOWN – 1, Dowager; 2, Easel; 3, Sheer-legs; 4, Nail; 5, Deep-laid; 6, Width; 7, Caduceus; 8, Method; 14, Nitrogen; 16, Energetic; 17, Flash-gun; 18, Ordain; 20, Lottery; 22, Potty; 24, Ariel; 25, Bolt.

No. 13

ACROSS – 1, Tapestry; 5, Tendon; 10, Crossword puzzle; 11, Imprest; 12, Chianti; 13, Gradient; 15, Eaves; 18, Hedge; 20, Ridicule; 23, Replica; 25, Founder; 26, The back of beyond; 27, Scythe; 28, Shottery.

DOWN – 1, Tocsin; 2, Prospered; 3, Suspend; 4, Roost; 6, Erudite; 7, Dozen; 8, Neediest; 9, Educated; 14, Earmarks; 16, Velodrome; 17, Charites; 19, Epitaph; 21, Crudest; 22, Friday; 24, Poesy; 25, Fifth.

No. 14

ACROSS – 1, Puritans; 5, Spider; 10, Realm; 11, Trevelyan; 12, Interbred; 13, Canto; 14, Apostil; 16, Dreamy; 19, Astern; 21, Settler; 23, Padua; 25, Unitarian; 27, Ownership; 28, Balfe; 29, Breast; 30, Pretexts.

DOWN – 1, Partisan; 2, Reactions; 3, Tamar; 4, Natural; 6, Prescient; 7, Doyen; 8, Random; 9, Bended; 15, Thesaurus; 17, Multiplex; 18, Princess; 20, Nought; 21, Slipper; 22, Aplomb; 24, Dance; 26, Ambit.

No. 15

ACROSS – 1, Peremptory; 6, Scow; 9, Gulf Stream; 10, Omen; 12, Cake; 13, Astrodrome; 15, Detested; 16, Hostel; 18, Losers; 20, Party-man; 23, Sparkling; 24, Echo; 26, Ella; 27, Billposter; 28, Type; 29, Tennis-ball.

DOWN – 1, Page; 2, Reliant; 3, Masterstroke; 4, Tar-water; 5, Rialto; 7, Compost; 8, Wonderland; 11, Top of the Pops; 14, Adolescent; 17, Pangolin; 19, Shallop; 21, Mahatma; 22, Finite; 25, Oral.

No. 16

ACROSS – 1, Wales; 4, Punch-bowl; 9, Sacred cow; 10, Buffs; 11, Waylay; 12, Zero hour; 14, Reasonable; 16, Toss; 19, Solo; 20, Pianoforte; 22, Politics; 23, Search; 26, Uncut; 27, Alexander; 28, Post-haste; 29, Lords.

DOWN – 1, Westwards; 2, Lucky; 3, Sheraton; 4, Pack; 5, New Zealand; 6, Hob-nob; 7, Off colour; 8, Laser; 13, Cabin class; 15, All Blacks; 17, Shepherds; 18, After all; 21, Stitch; 22, Plump; 24, Radar; 25, Peke.

No. 17

ACROSS – 1, Hydra; 4, Lost chord; 9, Patchouli; 10, Nodal; 11, Marriage-licence; 12, Nicety; 14, Hellenic; 17, Acrostic; 19, Peseta; 22, Eating one's terms; 24, Tokyo; 25, Hanseatic; 26, Nor'-wester; 27, Enrol.

DOWN – 1, Hypomania; 2, Deter; 3, Atheist; 4, Lounge; 5, Scillies; 6, Conical; 7, Ordinance; 8, Delve; 13, Caretaker; 15, Classical; 16, Ricochet; 18, Syncope; 20, Extreme; 21, Tenner; 22, Elton; 23, Rotor.

No. 18

ACROSS – 1, Craven; 4, Eftsoons; 10, Truepenny; 11, Betel; 12, Redcoat; 13, Norfolk; 14, Caleb; 15, Industry; 18, Straight; 20, Radio; 23, Enslave; 25, Hairpin; 26, Brent; 27, Dialectic; 28, Shagreen; 29, Beadle.

DOWN – 1, Cataract; 2, Arundel; 3, Euphorbia; 5, Flying Dutchman; 6, Sober; 7, Outdoor; 8, Saluki; 9, Knitting-needle; 16, Sortilege; 17, Corniche; 19, Tessera; 21, Deputed; 22, Lesbos; 24, Astir.

No. 19

ACROSS – 1, Stopped; 5, Acclaim; 9, Later; 10, Whitebait; 11, Caught; 12, Turncoat; 14, Obese; 15, Transient; 18, Substance; 20, Amain; 22, Tutoress; 24, Agnate; 26, Breathing; 27, Ratel; 28, Tung oil; 29, Endured.

DOWN – 1, Salacious; 2, Obtrude; 3, Parchment; 4, Down; 5, Acidulated; 6, Clean; 7, Anagoge; 8, Motet; 13, Standstill; 16, Staggered; 17, Tunnelled; 19, Bittern; 21, Alastor; 22, Tobit; 23, Ratio; 25, Ogee.

No. 20

ACROSS – 1, Silver screen; 9, Watchword; 10, Score; 11, Upshot; 12, Academic; 13, Turnip; 15, Porthole; 18, Covenant; 19, Drudge; 21, Tantalus; 23, Hecate; 26, Laura; 27, Reprobate; 28, Plaster saint.

DOWN – 1, Sawdust; 2, Lotus; 3, Ethiopian; 4, Spot; 5, Redactor; 6, Eased; 7, Wormwood; 8, Rescue; 14, Ravenous; 16, Torpedoes; 17, Enquires; 18, Cattle; 20, Element; 22, Avail; 24, Acari; 25, Epée.

No. 21

ACROSS – 1, Memsahib; 5, Hungry; 8, Drop anchor; 9, Thru; 10, Listed building; 11, Twoness; 13, In press; 15, Special; 18, Creates; 21, Cheshire cheese; 22, Ruth; 23, Impressive; 24, Jeeves; 25, Gossamer.

DOWN – 1, Mud-flat; 2, Moonstone; 3, Academe; 4, Incubus; 5, Hard-liner; 6, Nattier; 7, Rare gas; 12, Smash hits; 14, Extremism; 16, Picture; 17, Chekhov; 18, Cheerio; 19, Ephesus; 20, She-bear.

No. 22

ACROSS – 1, Caligula; 5, Eponym; 10, Moses; 11, April fool; 12, Rotterdam; 13, Abele; 14, Stumper; 16, Shindy; 19, Speech; 21, Damosel; 23, Radii; 25, Boardroom; 27, Goldsmith; 28, Curio; 29, Thirst; 30, Ganymede.

DOWN – 1, Compress; 2, Last trump; 3, Geste; 4, Leander; 6, Palladium; 7, Niobe; 8, Miller; 9, Grimes; 15, Premisses; 17, Discourse; 18, Old Moore; 20, Hobbit; 21, Drachma; 22, Bright; 24, Delhi; 26, Dicey.

No. 23

ACROSS – 1, Backchat; 5, Abound; 9, Contrive; 10, Crisis; 12, Loris; 13, Noiseless; 14, Fit as a fiddle; 18, Inconvenient; 21, Calendula; 23, Erica; 24, Opiate; 25, Kippered; 26, Arnold; 27, Entrepot.

DOWN – 1, Becalm; 2, Canard; 3, Christian; 4, Advantageous; 6, Burke; 7, Unsteady; 8, Disaster; 11, Dilapidation; 15, Innkeeper; 16, Cinchona; 17, Scullion; 19, Pirrip; 20, Daudet; 22, Natal.

No. 24

ACROSS – 1, Forgo; 4, Jack-knife; 9, Affluence; 10, Noise; 11, Skewer; 12, Diplomat; 14, Overcharge; 16, Stud; 19, Evil; 20, Republican; 22, Producer; 23, Ending; 26, Axiom; 27, Gargantua; 28, Delighted; 29, Nurse.

DOWN – 1, Flagstone; 2, Rifle; 3, Opulence; 4, Junk; 5, Chewing-gum; 6, Kindle; 7, Idiomatic; 8, Event; 13, Make-weight; 15, Editorial; 17, Denigrate; 18, Plantain; 21, Nutmeg; 22, Plaid; 24, Inter; 25, Bred.

No. 25

ACROSS – 1, Wassailer; 6, Roses; 9, Chasten; 10, Montana; 11, Sheaf; 12, Almshouse; 14, May; 15, Caterpillar; 17, Determinist; 19, Cam; 20, Ligaments; 22, Shrub; 24, Inertia; 26, Italics; 27, Tasso; 28, Precedent.

DOWN – 1, Wicks; 2, Stately; 3, Artificer; 4, Lancastrian; 5, Rum; 6, Ranch; 7, Seagull; 8, Snare-drum; 13, Marlinspike; 14, Medallist; 16, Intestate; 18, Tigress; 19, Carbine; 21, Motto; 23, Beset; 25, Asp.

No. 26

ACROSS – 1, Morose; 4, Pawnshop; 10, Sugar-loaf; 11, Idler; 12, Mildred; 13, Emerald; 14, Tired; 15, Altitude; 18, Porridge; 20, Wands; 23, Chelsea; 25, Recital; 26, Trail; 27, Inanimate; 28, Hard cash; 29, Trilby.

DOWN – 1, Messmate; 2, Regular; 3, Surf-rider; 5, Alfred the Great; 6, Naïve; 7, Halyard; 8, Parade; 9, Lords and ladies; 16, Town crier; 17, Psaltery; 19, Open air; 21, Netball; 22, Scotch; 24, Salic.

No. 27

ACROSS – 1, Pastel; 5, Linchpin; 9, Agitator; 10, Lagoon; 11, Treeless; 12, Elapse; 13, Endanger; 15, Aged; 17, Mope; 19, Symposia; 20, Ideals; 21, Normandy; 22, Nordic; 23, Tail-race; 24, Endorses; 25, Empire.

DOWN – 2, Angering; 3, Tottered; 4, Latter-day; 5, Lares and penates; 6, Crawler; 7, Prospero; 8, Nonsense; 14, Ex-service; 15, Alliance; 16, Endeared; 17, Malaprop; 18, Producer; 19, Soldier.

No. 28

ACROSS – 1, Pitch-and-toss; 9, Tobermory; 10, Bathe; 11, Lotion; 12, Pastoral; 13, Albeit; 15, Olympian; 18, Cockatoo; 19, Tragic; 21, Beam-ends; 23, Gorgon; 26, Slang; 27, Inamorata; 28, Trench mortar.

DOWN – 1, Patella; 2, Tobit; 3, Harmonica; 4, Nook; 5, Try-sails; 6, Sabot; 7, Starling; 8, Merlin; 14, Baccarat; 16, Marco Polo; 17, Mondrian; 18, Cubist; 20, Centaur; 22, Elgar; 24, Grant; 25, Wash.

No. 29

ACROSS – 1, Coincide; 5, Stalls; 10, Birds of a feather; 11, Lettice; 12, Bull Run; 13, Stagnate; 15, Refit; 18, Lodes; 20, Take away; 23, Terrier; 25, Pot-herb; 26, Parenthetically; 27, Silver; 28, Molested.

DOWN – 1, Cobble; 2, Irritated; 3, Casting; 4, Defoe; 6, Trawler; 7, Lehar; 8, Strength; 9, Off-break; 14, Autarchy; 16, Flageolet; 17, Platypus; 19, Science; 21, Article; 22, Obeyed; 24, Rural; 25, Putto.

No. 30

ACROSS – 1, Gainsaid; 5, Tandem; 10, Gully; 11, Philately; 12, Neglected; 13, Circe; 14, Illness; 16, Enigma; 19, Myself; 21, Retinue; 23, Allah; 25, Love-match; 27, Fine-drawn; 28, Peron; 29, Renown; 30, Geodesic.

DOWN – 1, Gigantic; 2, Illegally; 3, Style; 4, Impetus; 6, Anarchist; 7, Drear; 8, Mayhem; 9, Fiddle; 15, Eye-shadow; 17, Men-at-arms; 18, Mechanic; 20, Fulmar; 21, Revenge; 22, Gaffer; 24, Linen; 26, Moped.

No. 31

ACROSS – 1, Pipeclay; 5, Thames; 9, Earliest; 10, Mirror; 12, Thumb; 13, Moonshine; 14, Bowling-green; 18, Humanitarian; 21, Childhood; 23, Ivory; 24, Spirit; 25, Anathema; 26, Tinkle; 27, Peerless.

DOWN – 1, Pleats; 2, Porous; 3, Climb down; 4, Assimilation; 6, Heirs; 7, Martinet; 8, Sergeant; 11, Country dance; 15, Gladiator; 16, Thickset; 17, Ambition; 19, Cohere; 20, Bypass; 22, Drill.

No. 32

ACROSS – 1, Bonus; 4, Postcards; 9, Missioner; 10, Since; 11, Saddle; 12, Owl-light; 14, Eugene Aram; 16, Stir; 19, Lion; 20, Hellenises; 22, Gun-metal; 23, Bulbul; 26, Sight; 27, Tractable; 28, On the trot; 29, Droit.

DOWN – 1, Bombshell; 2, Nosed; 3, Swilling; 4, Punk; 5, Screw-balls; 6, Costly; 7, Runagates; 8, Sheet; 13, Malefactor; 15, Good night; 17, Resilient; 18, Unsuited; 21, Beetle; 22, Gusto; 24, Baboo; 25, Dart.

No. 33

ACROSS – 1, Chaperon; 9, Increase; 10, Fine; 11, Apple-blossom; 13, Mirage; 14, Laddered; 15, Testers; 16, Air-pump; 20, Accident; 22, Trains; 23, Question-mark; 25, Ibis; 26, Inactive; 27, Resigned.

DOWN – 2, Hair-line; 3, Pleasantries; 4, Reappear; 5, Nigella; 6, Scaled; 7, Mass; 8, Teamed up; 12, Sleep-walking; 15, Tranquil; 17, Intrados; 18, Minutiae; 19, Stunner; 21, Elicit; 24, Exam.

No. 34

ACROSS – 1, Bemuse; 4, Hastings; 10, Canvasser; 11, Piton; 12, Breadth; 13, Servant; 14, Tasso; 15, Cotswold; 18, Beanpole; 20, Refit; 23, Fig-leaf; 25, Oxonian; 26, Irish; 27, Irregular; 28, Etherise; 29, Brassy.

DOWN – 1, Backbite; 2, Manners; 3, Stand down; 5, Across the board; 6, Taper; 7, Netball; 8, Sanity; 9, As the crow flies; 16, Warmonger; 17, Sting-ray; 19, English; 21, Foibles; 22, Office; 24, Esher.

No. 35

ACROSS – 1, Flash; 4, Attention; 9, Epaulette; 10, Befit; 11, Benefit of clergy; 12, Annexe; 14, Shortage; 17, Derelict; 19, Absent; 22, Star of Bethlehem; 24, Omits; 25, Appertain; 26, Contender; 27, Cadet.

DOWN – 1, Free-board; 2, Amain; 3, Halifax; 4, Astute; 5, Twelfths; 6, Nebular; 7, Infuriate; 8, Natty; 13, Narration; 15, Estaminet; 16, Scabbard; 18, Look-see; 20, Baldric; 21, Stupor; 22, Stoic; 23, Hoard.

No. 36

ACROSS – 1, Freudian slip; 9, Millstone; 10, Olive; 11, Litter; 12, Odysseus; 13, Samian; 15, Dalmatia; 18, Push-over; 19, Scorch; 21, Dark blue; 23, Coffer; 26, April; 27, Full house; 28, Maiden speech.

DOWN – 1, Females; 2, Eclat; 3, Desperado; 4, Avon; 5, Stendhal; 6, Irons; 7, Director; 8, Red Sea; 14, Miserere; 16, Microchip; 17, Rebuffed; 18, Pedlar; 20, Harlech; 22, Bella; 24, Flute; 25, Plan.

No. 37

ACROSS – 1, Rampart; 5, Monocle; 9, Rinse; 10, Abundance; 11, Envoys; 12, Annalist; 14, Horse; 15, Foursomes; 18, Whole-meal; 20, Idiot; 22, Catholic; 24, Closer; 26, Lubricant; 27, Osric; 28, Burmese; 29, Admiral.

DOWN – 1, Raree-show; 2, Miniver; 3, Acetylene; 4, Tray; 5, Mournfully; 6, Nadia; 7, Confirm; 8, Erect; 13, Effeminate; 16, Still-room; 17, Satirical; 19, October; 21, Insurer; 22, Caleb; 23, Olive; 25, Stoa.

No. 38

ACROSS – 1, Tiresome; 5, Afghan; 10, Libya; 11, Geologist; 12, Goldfinch; 13, Patio; 14, Arizona; 16, Raisin; 19, Onager; 21, Matinee; 23, Robin; 25, Silliness; 27, Potassium; 28, Aspen; 29, Danish; 30, Integral.

DOWN – 1, Telegram; 2, Rebellion; 3, Scarf; 4, Magenta; 6, Footprint; 7, Hoist; 8, Notion; 9, Gopher; 15, Organists; 17, Innkeeper; 18, Personal; 20, Ruskin; 21, Milkman; 22, Tripod; 24, Baton; 26, Irate.

No. 39

ACROSS – 1, Dressage; 5, Old Vic; 9, Carousel; 10, Oberon; 12, Mused; 13, Satellite; 14, Guy Mannering; 18, Merchantable; 21, Arch-fiend; 23, Gloss; 24, Tablet; 25, Distance; 26, Estate; 27, Tennyson.

DOWN – 1, Decamp; 2, Egress; 3, Sourdough; 4, Grease monkey; 6, Libel; 7, Virginia; 8, Converge; 11, Standard time; 15, Enlighten; 16, Embattle; 17, Brickbat; 19, Mounts; 20, Astern; 22, Fleet.

No. 40

ACROSS – 1, Shako; 4, Limelight; 9, Overtaken; 10, Meant; 11, Turnip; 12, Ugliness; 14, All the same; 16, Chum; 19, Lawn; 20, Sign-writer; 22, Veracity; 23, Across; 26, Usage; 27, Name-plate; 28, Treatment; 29, Twist.

DOWN – 1, Shortfall; 2, Ameer; 3, Outright; 4, Lake; 5, Management; 6, Limpid; 7, Grapeshot; 8, Titus; 13, Assistance; 15, Lowercase; 17, Mare's-nest; 18, Crackpot; 21, Accent; 22, Vault; 24, Okapi; 25, Emit.

No. 41

ACROSS – 1, Goodness; 9, Cross-tie; 10, Dons; 11, Chastisement; 13, Utopia; 14, Lampreys; 15, Bruiser; 16, African; 20, Levanter; 22, Noggin; 23, Grey squirrel; 25, Odds; 26, Milanese; 27, Rallying.

DOWN – 2, Odometer; 3, Disciplinary; 4, Escalate; 5, Scuttle; 6, Possum; 7, Stye; 8, Jettison; 12, Morning glory; 15, Ball-game; 17, Funereal; 18, Abingdon; 19, Cruiser; 21, Toques; 24, Ella.

No. 42

ACROSS – 1, Strabo; 4, Estoppel; 10, Constable; 11, Orson; 12, Agitate; 13, Harriet; 14, Larch; 15, Vortices; 18, Bubastis; 20, Ozone; 23, Testudo; 25, Uncover; 26, Lhasa; 27, Cassowary; 28, Creamery; 29, Ostend.

DOWN – 1, Sociable; 2, Rentier; 3, Batrachia; 5, Shepherd's purse; 6, Odour; 7, Pastime; 8, Lenity; 9, Observation car; 16, Iron Cross; 17, Betrayed; 19, Upstage; 21, Obviate; 22, Italic; 24, Unarm.

No. 43

ACROSS – 1, Zero option; 6, Hemp; 9, Unsociable; 10, Mete; 12, Brae; 13, Margarine; 15, Identity; 16, Piglet; 18, Turban; 20, Villager; 23, Expletive; 24, Nome; 26, Avid; 27, Incinerate; 28, Yoga; 29, Progenitor.

DOWN – 1, Zeus; 2, Reserve; 3, Orchestrated; 4, Team-mate; 5, Oilers; 7, Ezekiel; 8, Prefecture; 11, Magic lantern; 14, Little Mary; 17, Riveting; 19, Ripping; 21, Gymnast; 22, Dinner; 25, Rear.

No. 44

ACROSS – 1, Galligaskins; 9, Israelite; 10, Siena; 11, Kidnap; 12, Choleric; 13, Negate; 15, Buddleia; 18, Marocain; 19, Icarus; 21, Grimaces; 23, Orison; 26, Track; 27, Immanence; 28, Sweet-william.

DOWN – 1, Griskin; 2, Lurid; 3, Inelastic; 4, Acis; 5, Keelhaul; 6, Nasal; 7, Hear hear; 8, Fascia; 14, Germinal; 16, Doctrinal; 17, Lifeline; 18, Mighty; 20, Sunbeam; 22, Askew; 24, Sinai; 25, Smew.

No. 45

ACROSS – 1, Dilemma; 5, Assumed; 9, Hamburger; 10, Talon; 11, Idiot; 12, Arboretum; 14, Thick as thieves; 17, Bacteriologist; 21, Explained; 23, Nurse; 24, Voter; 25, Cormorant; 26, Ringlet; 27, Suspend.

DOWN – 1, Dahlia; 2, Lumpish; 3, Moustache; 4, Aggravation; 5, Air; 6, Satyr; 7, Molotov; 8, Dynamism; 13, Battledores; 15, Ingenious; 16, Observer; 18, Capstan; 19, Surname; 20, Vetted; 22, Aural; 25, Cat.

No. 46

ACROSS – 1, Seascape; 5, Plater; 10, Field; 11, Alarmists; 12, Spadework; 13, Doyen; 14, Addison; 16, Locker; 19, Harris; 21, Pass out; 23, Angst; 25, Half-crown; 27, Neighbour; 28, Brier; 29, Timbre; 30, Doorstep.

DOWN – 1, Safe seat; 2, Alexandra; 3, Cadge; 4, Platoon; 6, Lame ducks; 7, Tasty; 8, Rising; 9, Jackal; 15, Stretcher; 17, Economist; 18, Eton crop; 20, School; 21, Palermo; 22, Walnut; 24, Grimm; 26, Caber.

No. 47

ACROSS – 1, Joystick; 9, Inherent; 10, Here; 11, Professional; 13, Stream; 14, Incident; 15, Prudery; 16, Embargo; 20, Porpoise; 22, Resort; 23, Nomenclature; 25, Arno; 26, Alfresco; 27, Residual.

DOWN – 2, Operator; 3, Shepherd's pie; 4, Informer; 5, Kinetic; 6, Physic; 7, Mean; 8, Stiletto; 12, Old man's beard; 15, Popinjay; 17, Marquess; 18, Gardenia; 19, Senator; 21, Incise; 24, Miff.

No. 48

ACROSS – 1, Alice; 4, Title-deed; 9, Logarithm; 10, Imago; 11, Haters; 12, Escorial; 14, Newspapers; 16, Kind; 19, Etty; 20, Wise virgin; 22, Careless; 23, Stalag; 26, Irate; 27, Orchestra; 28, Polyester; 29, Sieve.

DOWN – 1, All change; 2, Ingot; 3, Eardrops; 4, Tito; 5, Time-server; 6, Edison; 7, Examining; 8, Droll; 13, Spoil-sport; 15, Waterfall; 17, Denigrate; 18, Mistress; 21, Allege; 22, Crimp; 24, Lathe; 25, Scar.

No. 49

ACROSS – 1, Pitot; 4, Provinces; 9, Tangerine; 10, Final; 11, Nutcracker Suite; 12, Assume; 14, Studying; 17, Exterior; 19, Bourse; 22, Gentlemen-at-arms; 24, Tosti; 25, Narrowing; 26, Disagreed; 27, Susan.

DOWN – 1, Potentate; 2, Tenet; 3, Theorem; 4, Prince; 5, Overeats; 6, Infused; 7, Conciliar; 8, Solve; 13, Satanists; 15, Grease-gun; 16, Commence; 18, Rolling; 20, Options; 21, Snared; 22, Gated; 23, Ruins.

No. 50

ACROSS – 1, Regime; 4, Falsetto; 10, Plaintiff; 11, Untie; 12, Benefit; 13, Infanta; 14, Indus; 15, Riddance; 18, Debonair; 20, Cabin; 23, Brigade; 25, Educate; 26, Extra; 27, Inebriate; 28, Spectral; 29, Adroit.

DOWN – 1, Republic; 2, Grained; 3, Manifesto; 5, Auf Wiedersehen; 6, Stuff; 7, Titanic; 8, One-way; 9, Victoria Regina; 16, Accoutred; 17, Interest; 19, Epistle; 21, Bravado; 22, Abbess; 24, Await.

No. 51

ACROSS – 1, March hare; 6, Moses; 9, Cabaret; 10, Timpani; 11, Ahead; 12, Cimmerian; 14, Ray; 15, Tickled pink; 17, Poets' Corner; 19, Fur; 20, Intervene; 22, Genoa; 24, Abutted; 26, Inboard; 27, Diego; 28, Pigheaded.

DOWN – 1, Mecca; 2, Rubbery; 3, Herodotus; 4, Anticyclone; 5, Eft; 6, Mamie; 7, Swahili; 8, Spinnaker; 13, Malingering; 14, Reprimand; 16, Dirigible; 18, Enthuse; 19, Finland; 21, Ratio; 23, Added; 25, Dip.

No. 52

ACROSS – 1, Dupin; 4, Ampersand; 9, Sweetmeat; 10, Ledge; 11, Insect; 12, Integral; 14, Second mate; 16, Soup; 19, Lamb; 20, Lack-lustre; 22, Forecast; 23, Gillie; 26, Calve; 27, Dramatist; 28, Dead march; 29, Ended.

DOWN – 1, Dismissal; 2, Pleas; 3, Noticing; 4, Aged; 5, Put-and-take; 6, Roller; 7, Adderwort; 8, Dwell; 13, Ambassador; 15, Camarilla; 17, Presented; 18, Ruminate; 21, Scream; 22, Faced; 24, Laird; 25, Dash.

No. 53

ACROSS – 1, Médoc; 4, Trump card; 9, Landscape; 10, Nadir; 11, Sheba; 12, Fourpenny; 13, Old Bill; 15, Lending; 18, Bustard; 20, Put down; 21, Big dipper; 23, Rebel; 25, Grave; 26, Out of form; 27, Steel band; 28, Timon.

DOWN – 1, Mills bomb; 2, Dance; 3, Costa Rica; 4, Tearful; 5, Unequal; 6, Pin-up; 7, Andantino; 8, Darcy; 14, Designate; 16, Net profit; 17, Gentlemen; 19, Diploma; 20, Pirated; 21, Bogus; 22, Ideal; 24, Bloom.

No. 54

ACROSS – 1, Phosphate; 6, Sodom; 9, Rubbish; 10, Gearbox; 11, Yield; 12, Egg-beater; 13, Intrepid; 15, Snip; 19, Eyas; 20, Hell-bent; 23, Cold-frame; 24, Girth; 26, Amnesia; 27, Vertigo; 28, Posit; 29, Earthwork.

DOWN – 1, Party-line; 2, Ombre; 3, Prie-dieu; 4, Athletic; 5, Engage; 6, Stayer; 7, Debutante; 8, Mixer; 14, Tramlines; 16, Pitchfork; 17, Receiver; 18, Oligarch; 21, Offset; 22, Carafe; 23, Cramp; 25, Rhino.

No. 55

ACROSS – 1, Write off; 5, Scuffs; 10, A Christmas Carol; 11, Turkish; 12, Implore; 13, Uttering; 15, Thong; 18, Arran; 20, Corvette; 23, Kitties; 25, Hopeful; 26, Vancouver Island; 27, Reeled; 28, Headgear.

DOWN – 1, Wealth; 2, Inheritor; 3, Edifice; 4, Fetch; 6, Cockpit; 7, Forgo; 8, Selvedge; 9, Malinger; 14, Incisive; 16, Out-of-date; 17, Walk-over; 19, Noisome; 21, Exposed; 22, Glider; 24, Tinge; 25, Horse.

No. 56

ACROSS – 1, Tamarisk; 5, Abused; 9, Grievous; 10, Pavlov; 12, Rotor; 13, Hexagonal; 14, Interrogator; 18, Slave-drivers; 21, Hamstring; 23, Asian; 24, Dodder; 25, Inedible; 26, Laputa; 27, Cardigan.

DOWN – 1, Tagore; 2, Moiety; 3, Reverence; 4, South Georgia; 6, Bhang; 7, Salinity; 8, De Valera; 11, Extravaganza; 15, Garlanded; 16, Asphodel; 17, Warmed up; 19, Kitbag; 20, Intern; 22, Trent.

No. 57

ACROSS – 1, Object; 5, Werewolf; 9, Accusative; 10, Toga; 11, Antelope; 12, Ogress; 13, Gala; 15, Scimitar; 18, Side-slip; 19, Peel; 21, Oswald; 23, Language; 25, Mica; 26, Echinoderm; 27, Assignee; 28, Sodden.

DOWN – 2, Bacon; 3, Enumerate; 4, Teapot; 5, Whited sepulchre; 6, Rhetoric; 7, Water; 8, Legislate; 14, Amidships; 16, Impounded; 17, Bludgeon; 20, Ananas; 22, Amati; 24, Gorse.

No. 58

ACROSS – 1, Woodpecker; 6, Edge; 10, Upturns; 11, Putting; 12, Duplicate; 13, Ralph; 14, Token; 15, Dismissal; 17, Manhandle; 20, Gloss; 21, Let-up; 23, Fee simple; 25, Phaeton; 26, Tottery; 27, Erne; 28, Derailment.

DOWN – 1, Wound; 2, Outspoken; 3, Persian carpets; 4, Costard; 5, Express; 7, Drill; 8, Eggshells; 9, Starting-pistol; 14, Time-lapse; 16, Show-piece; 18, Defence; 19, Electra; 22, Train; 24, Egypt.

No. 59

ACROSS – 1, Stickler; 9, Epigraph; 10, Lien; 11, Scene-shifter; 13, Stares; 14, Implicit; 15, Triplet; 16, Platoon; 20, Litigate; 22, Feeble; 23, Grantchester; 25, Twit; 26, Asteroid; 27, Spending.

DOWN – 2, Trimeter; 3, Conscription; 4, Licensee; 5, Reverie; 6, Bishop; 7, Part; 8, Sheraton; 12, Faint-hearted; 15, Telegram; 17, Lifetime; 18, Oblation; 19, Legends; 21, Anchor; 24, Acts.

No. 60

ACROSS – 1, Kenite; 4, Banausic; 10, Noumena; 11, Growler; 12, Marcescent; 13, Smee; 15, Kinetic; 17, Titanic; 19, Robeson; 21, Natasha; 23, Maro; 24, Objets d'art; 27, Miasmal; 28, Aboukir; 29, Roestone; 30, Fenrir.

DOWN – 1, King-maker; 2, Neutron; 3, Trecentist; 5, Aeginetan; 6, Amok; 7, Solomon; 8, Corfe; 9, Banc; 14, Statoscope; 16, Cunobelin; 18, Chatterer; 20, Burbage; 22, Spanker; 23, Mimir; 25, Elah; 26, Omit.

ACROSS

1 Judges chapter 4, verses 17 to 22. Jael, the wife of Heber the **KENITE**, hit the nail on the head of Sisera.

4 SI is the abbreviation of Système International, so 'A universal international system' = A U SI in B A N C (answer to 9 Down) gives us that delightfully snobbish word **BANAUSIC**.

10 A possible pronunciation of **NOUMENA** being now-men-a, the build-up is N O U ('Now, some say') + anagram of N A M E.

11 Growltiger is one of T. S. Eliot's Practical Cats, wooer of The Lady Griddlebone; after losing the game 'tig' he becomes **GROWLER** which can mean a small iceberg (see 17 Across) but here means a four-wheeled cab.

12 After M A R C (drink) E ('e) takes SCENT (the trail) = **MARCESCENT**.

13 One of Captain Hook's pirates in Peter Pan was **SMEE** ('s me = it is me, pirates being no grammarians).

15 If one is still, one lacks **KINETIC** energy.

17 No small iceberg (see 11 Across above) caused the **TITANIC** (great) disaster.

19 Paul **ROBESON**. With robes on, one is invested.

21 A S (like) H A (heavy artillery = big guns) led by N A T King Cole (American pianist and singer) = **NATASHA**.

23 Publius Vergilius **MARO** better known as Virgil, also called (from his birthplace) the Mantuan (Poet); 'the Great Man "tuan" continuously' = 'the Great Mantuan'.

24 Walter Savage Landor wrote 'Nature I loved, and, next to Nature, Art', so **OBJETS D'ART** would be Savage's beloved (if second-best) things.

27 L A M S (hits) A I M (object) backwards gives **MIASMAL**.

28 Nelson won the Battle of the Nile in the Bay of **ABOUKIR**. 'Honor est a Nilo' is a famous anagram of Horatio Nelson.

29 'line, say' = R O E (which sounds like row = line) + STONE (weight) = **ROESTONE** = oolite.

30 **FENRIR**, the dreaded wolf of Norse mythology. 'runs = R (as in bowling analyses), so 'one runs' = I R by (next to) FEN (marsh) and R (river).

DOWN

1 One of Edgar Wallace's Sanders of the River books is Sandi the **KING-MAKER**. A successful draughts player makes his piece into a king.

2 **NEUTRON** star. Anagram of 'run on E.T.'

137

3 See 'Giotto's O' in Brewer's Dictionary of Phrase and Fable or other reference book. **TRECENTIST** is an artist of the fourteenth century, Giotto being a famous example.

5 **AEGINETAN** Marbles (or Sculptures) found in the island of Aegina. E G IN (Oriental spirit) in anagram of A NEAT.

6 One is deranged to run **AMOK** but 'am OK' = 'nothing wrong with me'.

7 Monday's child is fair of face. **SOLOMON** Grundy. Born on a Monday.

8 C (100 = many) ORFE (a goldfish) in **CORFE** Castle.

9 **BANC**, the judges' bench 'whence justice is dispensed' sounds like 'bank' whence money is dispensed.

14 **STATOSCOPE**, anagram of 'poet's Tosca'.

16 **CUNOBELIN** or Cymbeline, old British king. C (caught) UNN ('Joshua's father craftily' anagram of NUN, father of biblical Joshua) holding OBELI the printer's 'daggers'.

18 Mad HATTER in CE (Church of England = 'church') + R (right) = **CHATTERER** = 'talkative bird'.

20 Richard **BURBAGE** Shakespearian actor and name of village in Wiltshire.

22 **SPANKER** = a fast horse and also = a sail (clued as 'sale's sound').

23 The real name of Mimi in La Boheme was Lucia, so MIMI (Lucia's alias) + R (right) = **MIMIR**, in Norse mythology the guardian of the fountain of wisdom.

25 David slew Goliath in the valley of **ELAH** (I Sam. 17) a place the reverse of 'hale' or healthy for his victim.

26 **OMIT** (neglect) anagram of M (thousand) TO I (to one).